Getting My Ducks in a Row

and Other Stories of Faith

You are loved by
a gracious God!

Love, Gaye Lindfors

Gaye Lindfors

I couldn't wait to read this new book of Gaye's, and I loved every page. With raw honesty and humor, Gaye uses her remarkable gift of words to unlock amazing life lessons in this book. I laughed and cried as I caught a glimpse of the heart of God for me through these pages. You will want this book for yourself and for gifts for others too.

PASTOR LONDA LUNDSTROM
The Father's House, Burnsville, MN

Delightful. Inspiring. Motivating. You'll love Gaye's warm, welcoming and witty writing style while relaxing into her call for a deeper closeness with God. Read it cover to cover or one little section per day. Either way, you'll emerge smiling and better equipped to enjoy your life to the full. Bravo!

MARNIE SWEDBERG, international speaker & leadership mentor
author of 13 books, www.Marnie.com

Gaye's charming and humorous way of looking at life will make you feel right at home, as if you're having a cup of coffee with a good friend who is telling you a great story with a lesson that she has learned. As women we can often tell ourselves we need to have it all together while thinking we're not enough, and Gaye shares stories of having grace with others and even ourselves, as we see life through God's eyes where He gently reminds us He is enough.

PAULETTE KUTZLER, radio host

Gaye writes with truth, candor, humor, and authenticity. She lovingly draws you in as an exceptional storyteller. If you need encouragement in juggling all the multi-tasking you have to do, this book is for you. You will be greatly encouraged as Gaye invites you to God's word through all you are facing in this ever-changing world.

DONNA FAGERSTROM, speaker, author, ministry wife

God has blessed Gaye with an incredible gift of storytelling that reaches far beyond the ordinary. With raw reality, tender truth and a generous measure of humor, she not only reaches you right where you are at, but invites you to journey with her through the good, the not so good and the just plain "ugly duckling" days of our lives. Believing God sees us through grace-filled eyes, she challenges us to join her in freely admitting our faults, addressing our flaws and refreshing our faith in the God who has it all under control. Thank you, Gaye; you have once again allowed your beautifully penned words to touch hearts and impact lives for His glory.

ALICIA SCHEMPER ("Alicia from Sheldon")
friend, sister in Christ

Gaye has a beautiful inviting writing style drawing us in with each honest heartfelt sentence. Getting our ducks in a row is a long time saying and a legacy of shoulds. Step into several life stories that invite us to breathe in the journey. God just wants to do more with our lives than we can imagine. There will be issues, struggles, ducks not lining up - even swimming in different ponds - but there is joy found in the presence of God's power. Grab a cup of coffee - experience peace, humor, inspiration. Reflect on your story within the messages of "Getting My Ducks in a Row and Other Stories of Faith."

SUE LENNARTSON, life coach, over 30 years in ministry
author, speaker, child of God

Gaye Lindfors' new book, captures the art of storytelling. Each story is drizzled with hope and humor and told in a way that will encourage the reader to expect good things in their future. This positive, energizing, and hope-filled read is hard to put down.

TRACEY MITCHELL, author, television host

Gaye Lindfors has done it again. She has put a smile on my face and a chuckle in my heart. This book is a fun, relatable read that will drive you to not only love the author and her authenticity, but it will also encourage you to love yourself and be drawn to God in a more authentic, intimate way. If you're looking for a positive read - this is it.

WENDIE PETT, health and wellness expert,
TV show host of *Visibly Fit*, www.wendiepett.com

Gaye Lindfors is a masterful storyteller. She takes ordinary life experiences and shines a light on the Living God, as no one else can do. In her book, Gaye shows us how to find joy and peace in our pond moments instead of fretting over finding the right ducks, the right pond and putting them in an imaginary row. Her message is bathed in love, mercy, grace, and a bit of Gaye Lindfors humor.

SUE Z. MCGRAY, author of *Becoming Visible*
www.suezmcgray.com

Gaye's writings encourage me and give me hope for my days! They lift me up, reminding me of God's steady care and love.

MARY GRACE from Arizona, friend

In a time where there is a new normal and overriding fears are in all our lives, this book will make you laugh and bring you joy. You will discover new confidence to face your challenges and see the strength it produces in you. Gaye has a wonderful way of experiencing daily moments with such enthusiasm for life that you will be encouraged to do the same.

DR. MARINA MCLEAN, Mega Women

Gaye Lindfors has a delightful way of telling stories in a way that everyone can relate to. When you read Gaye's stories, you think to yourself, "something like that happened to me too!" — which draws you in closer to the important messages she is teaching us. Each chapter is an important reminder of God's love and grace for us. This book is filled with humor, joy, and hope, and is the perfect gift for your friends and family.

HOLLY ZELINSKY, CEO Nationally Speaking, Inc.

Gaye's new book is both humorous and relatable. She takes you on a journey through every day experiences reminding us that we are loved and cared for by God in the big and small moments. Gaye also has a way of breaking down passages of Scripture into bite-sized pieces that bring the Bible to life!

CARRIE ROBAINA
host of *She Walks in Truth* podcast

Gaye's book is just delightful and practical with the teaching insight she provides to wrap up each story. Thank you, Gaye, for making me smile, over and over, as I read and enjoyed your stories and each lesson!

KIMBERLY NYBORG
radio host, speaker, and writer

Getting My Ducks in a Row and Other Stories of Faith

Unless otherwise noted, scripture quotations are from the NIV Women of Faith Study Bible, New International Version. Scripture taken from the HOLY BIBLE, NEW INTERNATIONAL VERSION®. Copyright © 1973, 1978, 1984 International Bible Society. Used by permission of Zondervan Publishing House. All rights reserved.

The "NIV" and "New International Version" trademarks are registered in the United States Patent and Trademark Office by International Bible Society. Use of either trademark requires the permission of the International Bible Society.

Scripture taken from THE MESSAGE, designated The Message, are from THE MESSAGE REMIX: The Bible in Contemporary Language by Eugene H. Peterson. Copyright © 1993, 1994, 1995, 1996, 2000, 2001, 2002. Used by permission of NavPress Publishing Group.

Scripture quotations marked NLT are taken from the Holy Bible, New Living Translation, copyright © 1996, 2004, 2007 by Tyndale House Foundation. Used by permission of Tyndale House Publishers, Inc., Carol Stream, Illinois 60188. All rights reserved.

Scripture quotations marked CSB have been taken from the Christian Standard Bible®. Copyright ©2017 by Holman Bible Publishers. Used by permission. Christian Standard Bible® and CSB® are federally registered trademarks of Holman Bible Publishers.

ISBN: 9798562646606

Printed in the United States of America

Cover design, typesetting, and book design: Stephanie Hofhenke & Terri Olson STRING Marketing, Inc.

Getting My Ducks in a Row

and Other Stories of Faith

For Steve

*You have helped me find my ducks, gather my ducks,
and have been my biggest supporter
when I try and get them in a row.*

*Thank you for listening, encouraging, and loving me.
You have significantly shaped my faith,
and you've shown me how to love people well.*

*I couldn't ask for a better person to do life with.
You're my guy.*

Table of Contents

Foreword by Dawn Barton

I always cringe a little when I tell people this because it's ridiculously cliched and wonderfully true… JOY IS A CHOICE. Joy, it's a choice and a gift. Just like waking up in the morning and choosing to put on those deliciously comfy yoga pants that have never actually been to yoga, we have to make a conscious choice to seek joy every day because Joy is God, and God is joy.

Now imagine just for a moment that God is like the master conductor of our lives. He draws together unique sounds and instruments to create a sort of harmony, and when all the right pieces come into place, life becomes a majestic, joyful symphony. It's filled with high notes and low notes, hard times, and good times. Bad relationships we learn from, and good ones that nourish our soul and fill our "joy cup." If we let God, and we pay close attention, we will see God's precious gifting of people right when we need them most. Gaye Lindfors is a beautiful piece of my life's joyful symphony.

God's gift of Gaye came in the form of an Instagram message. A small, simple message that would spark a cherished friendship. Her wisdom and words are precious gifts to me almost daily, and I know they will be for you as you read through this book. Gaye makes me laugh, and her joy bursts through these pages like bright rays of sunshine during a dreary day.

I suspect that you will feel as I have; Gaye wrote this book for me. She knew my struggles, and she wrote a whole book just for me. My ducks are wild and never in a row. I struggle with my need to control those crazed ducks and forget to give it God, seek him, and in that seeking find the joy He intended for me. These pages, these stories of faith, reminded me that He is in control, and if I let him, He will conduct the most glorious and joyful symphony of my life.

Dawn Barton
WRITER | SPEAKER | JOYOLOGIST

A Note from Gaye

Hey, friend!

I can call you friend, right? I mean, you sure will know something about me after you read these stories. And I already know a few things about you, too. You enjoy reading. You picked up this book, right? You love a good giggle, and you, too, have an interest in this God I love so much. So, we already have some things in common! I think that makes us friends. Aren't we lucky?

So, friend, can I just say…
Life is really, really good. In fact, most of the time, it is exceptionally good.

I believe there are hundreds of little blessings that show up on our path every single day … the sun will come up tomorrow, and the new day brings renewed hope. I believe that words and people and moments and colors and laughter are what make life EXCITING and EXTRAORDINARY.

And when I'm in my I-know-this-isn't-likely-but-I'm-choosing-to-believe-it-anyway world, I also believe that the Minnesota Vikings will one day win the Super Bowl. I believe that there are no bad calories in sea salt, milk chocolate-covered caramels. And arms and thighs that jiggle will one day be a fashion statement.

Yes. Life is good. And…
Sometimes, we make mistakes. We say things and do things

that make us wonder ... *Really? Why did I think that was a good idea?* Disappointments and broken dreams bump into our Happy Place and our colorful world becomes drabby grey. Decisions are made that we have no control over, but they wreak havoc in our life. Trying to get our ducks in a row is a herculean task that leaves us exhausted. Everything seems messed up.

Oh, friend, we've all been there.

However...
Hang with me. There is hope.
You can always start again.
You may want to lean in a bit closer here because this is really good news...
God is a God of start-agains.

One of my favorite Bible passages reminds us of this...

> This is what God says, the God who builds a road right through the ocean, who carves a path through pounding waves ... 'Forget about what's happened; don't keep going over old history. Be alert, be present. **I'm about to do something brand-new**. It's bursting out! Don't you see it? There it is! I'm making a road through the desert, rivers in the badlands.'

Yes! In my attempt to try and get my act together, fix things, and keep control of situations, I forget that God is a God of grace. Love. Restoration. I don't need to get all my ducks in a row for Him to do something brand new in my life. Isn't this a great realization?

We're going to have some fun in these pages! I'm not afraid

to point out my own mishaps, and I find it ridiculously easy to laugh at myself. If you've been reading my blog, a few of the stories may be familiar. They captured moments that were so memorable, or fun, that I wanted to share them again with some additional perspective.

Words from a few of my favorite authors are included in these notes of encouragement, along with stories and promises from The Good Book. They are referenced in the "Notes" section at the back of the book so you can check them out. And I know you're going to love the images I've included! You can download them (in color!) at www. GayeLindfors.com/images.

As I've unapologetically noted in my other books, sometimes I use fancy, impressive phrases and words like "*Good grief*!" and "*Ugh*!" I've never found better, or more easily understood, words to replace these from-the-gut expressions. They roll off my tongue so naturally, and feel so good, I just keep using them. "Ooftah" is still my favorite word, and I know that I frustrate many of my Norwegian friends when I don't spell it correctly − "Uff da."

You'll find a few themes in these stories. My deep love for family. A passion for books. Mega doses of gratitude to God. An uncanny inability to get my ducks in a row. And a delightful desire to find humor in daily living.

Thank you so much for stopping by to share a slice of life, together. You matter. You are loved.

Gaye Lindfors
October 1, 2020, St. Paul, MN

1

S.O.S. Flares and Faith

Choose faith in a loving, powerful God, rather than fussing over what you cannot control or fix.

Fear stops my breathing and causes an ugly red rash to creep up my neck.

This apprehension is my fear of being caught in a storm at sea. Or on a lake. Or even a backyard pond.

I have no intention of ever being in a situation where I have to whack seagulls on the head with a paddle to secure my lunch, all the while clinging to slimy strands of seaweed!

Perhaps my past experiences have created this almost irrational fear of being lost in the middle of a body of water in a storm, with the boat capsizing in **it's never been this bad** proportion.

There was the canoe incident at Camp Fire Girls Camp when I was ten years old. I was taking the tip-your-canoe-over-on-purpose qualifying exam to prove that I could save myself. Who in their right mind thought this was a good idea? On that particular afternoon, storm clouds came rolling in, and rain descended. I couldn't open my eyes because the rain pellets hurt like they were puncturing my eyeballs. Did I mention I was in the water, in the middle of the lake, clinging to the side of the canoe? I gulped at minimum 32 gallons of lake water while trying to keep my head above the waves. I'm drowning, and the lifeguard is just standing on the shore with her clipboard, monitoring my progress.

Then there was the sailboat incident in the Madeline Islands with a group of friends. Darkest clouds and strongest winds I'd ever seen. The horizontal rain pelted us as we clung to the handrails in our little life jackets, all leaning to one side, just like our sailboat. Even our rent-a-captain thought we were going to die.

So, yeah. Boating is not my Happy Place.

That's why I find the story of Jesus calming the storm in the fourth chapter of Mark both horrifying and remarkable.

Mark describes the scene like this:

> That day when evening came, he [Jesus] said to his disciples, 'Let us go over to the other side.' Leaving the crowd behind, they took him along, just as he was, in the boat. There were also other boats with him. A furious squall came up, and the waves broke over the boat, so that it was nearly swamped. Jesus was in the stern, sleeping on a cushion. The disciples woke him and said to him, 'Teacher, don't you care if we drown?' He got up, rebuked the wind and said to the waves, 'Quiet! Be still!' Then the wind died down and it was completely calm. He said to his disciples, 'Why are you so afraid? Do you still have no faith?'

OK. Let's review.

Mark writes, "A furious squall came up." Well, doesn't that just sound peachy?

The "waves broke over the boat." This is not good, not good at all.

"So that it was nearly swamped." Right about then is when I'd start sending up the S.O.S. flares.

And where was Jesus? "Jesus was in the stern, sleeping on a cushion." With all due respect to Jesus, I would have said something, loudly, that probably verged on the hysterical.

(*"Really? You decide that now is a good time to take a nap?"*)
Oh me, of little faith.

I wonder why Mark wrote that Jesus was **sleeping on a cushion**. Maybe it's because this detail increases our awareness of how relaxed and non-stressed Jesus was during the furious squall? If water was coming over the sides, that cushion must have been a bit soggy. Yet, Jesus slept.

This story jumpstarts my faith battery – big time. Notice that Jesus was not hunched over in the boat, wringing his hands, whispering, "What should we do? Who has a book that tells us what to do in a furious squall with waves breaking over the boat? Does anyone get a cellphone signal here? I need to call my friend and ask him what we should do."

No. Jesus was sleeping. Resting. Without fear.

His heart could rest because He knew The One who was right there, riding out the storm with them. Every single day of his life, Jesus was focused on **The Father.**

Back to the disciples…

You get a clue that the disciples were clearly out of sorts when they suggested Jesus didn't care if they drowned. Wow. I mean, Really? They'd seen him cast out demons. Heal the sick. They'd heard him teach. He'd personally invited each one of them to travel and live with Him. And yet, they questioned how much He cared about them when the waters got rough.

But I get it. How the disciples felt. You, too? Fear has a way of strangling our faith if we allow it.

Turning our attention from the storm to The One who calms the storm requires faith. Faith requires trusting in and believing the God who is riding the waves with us. Faith means knowing He will never let us go, no matter how completely submerged in rough waters we are. Faith demands looking away from our situation and towards what we know God is able to do.

Oftentimes, our best lessons come from people who know storms well. Read these wise words from three of my favorite storm riders:

Author Kim Meeder writes,

> When we choose to focus on the storm, our despair and fear grow, and our trust in Jesus shrinks...
> Or, we can choose to come to our Lord within our personal storms and worship Him because He still redeems, He still loves and He is still God.

Great preacher and teacher Tony Evans has written a study Bible that has become one of my favorite study tools. In it, he defines faith as "Acting like God is telling the truth; acting like it is so even when it is not so in order that it might be so simply because God said so." Chew on those ideas for a bit!

In her book, *Believing God*, Beth Moore writes "Faith is never the denial of reality. It is belief in a greater reality ... Faith is not just something you have. It's something you do."

Some days feel like we're riding in a furious squall with out-of-our-control waves of difficulty and anxiety breaking over the boat. **God expects us to send up our S.O.S.**

flares. And then he expects us to find a cushion and rest, knowing He's taking care of the situation. His perfect way, in His perfect timing.

What does God not expect us to do in that squall? He does not expect us to heave ourselves over the side of the boat to struggle against the waves, gather our ducks together and line them up in a pretty little row, and then try and fix or control the storm!

We work so vigorously at trying to make every situation "right" – to make the storm ease up or go away. We want everything to feel orderly again, making sure life is tidy, if not perfect, and we have each situation under control. All the while, God is inviting us to stop fussing with our ducks and rest, on a cushion. **We can choose faith over fuss.**

Oh, we are so gloriously cared for, so consistently tended to, and so deeply loved by a caring, tender, and loving God. We can be content to choose faith instead of what-if's, rest instead of pacing, and trust instead of worry.

> Fear not, for I have redeemed you; I have summoned you by name; **you are mine**. When you pass through the waters, **I will be with you**; and when you pass through the rivers, **they will not sweep over you**. When you walk through the fire, **you will not be burned**; the flames will not set you ablaze ... **Do not be afraid, for I am with you.**

Now that's a promise we can cling to!

You may not even know where all your ducks are paddling today. That's OK.

Ducks were never meant to live every moment in a picture-perfect row.

You can choose faith in a loving, powerful God, instead of fussing over what you cannot control or fix.

Grab your cushion and rest, my friend. God's got this.

2

Catch a Glimpse

Bring a breath
of fresh air
and a glimpse of
the living God!

I was at one of my favorite Happy Places – The Minnesota State Fair.

The "Great Minnesota Get Together" is only the setting for this story, but I just can't keep from telling you how much I love this annual event. Mom and dad worked there for 50+ years every August, and my sisters and I grew up loving everything about the event-people, colors, music, shows, parades, animals, and the food, especially Sweet Martha's Cookies. Many of my best childhood memories are of living in the fair's campground in our camper school bus for three weeks each summer, helping mom and dad with their agricultural responsibilities and crop art shows, and being around many of the nicest people on earth.

Anyway. To my story!

I never miss going to the Minnesota State Fair, and attending one of the Grandstand shows with my friends, Mary and Mary, is always a highlight. A few years ago, we saw Frankie Valli and The Four Seasons perform. If you don't know who they are, bless you. When we saw him in concert, he was in his mid-80s. I know. He's been around for a long time. You will be older one day, too.

Let me give you a quick introduction ... Frankie Valli is an American entertainer known for his unusual tenor voice. He sings really, really high. Like falsetto high. Maybe you've heard some of his biggest hits – "*Can't Take My Eyes Off You,*" "*Walk Like a Man,*" "*Grease,*" "*Big Girls Don't Cry.*" Or perhaps you saw his musical autobiography "*Jersey Boys*" on stage, one of the best shows I've ever seen. Enter his name into your browser search bar, and you'll discover his incredible life story. The Four Seasons are his much younger, especially good-looking back-up group.

On that evening at the State Fair grandstand, Mary and Mary and I had fabulous seats on the plaza a few rows from the stage. I didn't know the woman sitting to my right, but let's call her Iris. She was **extraordinarily** excited to see Frankie, and her affection and devotion bubbled up profusely as she described to me her commitment to his music. For years, Iris has traveled the country attending his shows. She has all his albums. A monumental life event was when she met him in person years ago, and he kissed her on the cheek. She truly could not contain her enthusiasm.

We heard the announcement that the show was going to begin. The music that was hyping-up the crowd stopped, except for a soft drum-roll. The stage lights dimmed. Iris grabbed my arm, pointed to the back of the stage, and semi-whispered. "There he is! There he is!"

We could see Frankie Valli's silhouette far back in the corner of the stage. He was standing there very still, with only his shape obvious to us. The drama was enough to make Iris cry.

The show hadn't even started, but she had gotten a **glimpse** of her idol. And her glimpse prompted her to want to see more, know more, and experience more of who he was and what he had to offer. Her anticipation for the concert to come was exuberance defined.

Have you ever had a similar experience?

Think of those moments when you've caught a glimpse of someone, or something, that matters to you. You see someone you love walking out of the airport amid a mass of people. You're returning home and you turn down the road and see the corner of your childhood home. Your granddaughter is in the school play, singing in the chorus in the back row, so you crouch half-way up from the seat of your chair to sneak a peek at her.

However, you want more than the glimpse, don't you? You want to fully see and experience the person (or place or event) that has caught your eye. You stretch your neck to see around, or over, whomever is blocking your view. You push aside whatever is keeping you from encountering that important someone or thing. You want the promise of the glimpse.

A faith question that has caused me to thoughtfully and intentionally think about my life and how I show up in it is this – *When people see me, what do they catch a glimpse of*? Do my actions and words invite them to know more about the God I serve? Do I give them a peek into a joy- and faith-filled life? A life that loves people and trusts God's faithfulness? Or do they see a fretting- and complaint-filled life? A life with too many scenes of judging others while trusting in my own ability to get my ducks in a row?

This is what I want them to see:

> Go out into the world uncorrupted, **a breath of fresh air** in this squalid and polluted society. **Provide people with a glimpse of good living and of the living God**.

My sweet friend, the hurtful and unkind words being shouted from all corners of the world these days is extraordinary. The anger and messages of shame and blame that we and our loved ones are hearing are exceptionally sad and unsettling. The noise is deafening. Unfortunately, some of those messages come from Christ's followers. I think that is heartbreaking. What do people catch a glimpse of when they experience those strident messages?

And ... the world is flooded with messages of LOVE. ENCOURAGEMENT. Music and words that unite us and give us the courage to take another step.

We can show up for the Iris's in the world who have caught a glimpse of something wonderful and want more of it. More joy and more hope. We can give them a glimpse of forgiveness and a peaceful heart. We can give them a glimpse of the living God who LOVES us and everyone unconditionally.

Our lives can tell stories of redemption and restoration. Our words can bring peace and clarity. Our messages can offer truth that is bathed in love and mercy and grace. We Christians can show the world how to celebrate God's faithfulness. Through our actions, we can invite people to discover a God who is The King of Kings and Lord of Lords, yet knows how many hairs are on each person's head. Let's give them a glimpse of the living God!

This mindset does not ask us to abdicate our beliefs or promote a shallow faith full of compromise. It requires us to lead with love. Many of us grew up hearing this Bible verse:

> Jesus replied: 'Love the Lord your God with all your heart and with all your soul and with all your mind. This is the first and greatest commandment.'

And the second is like it: 'Love your neighbor as yourself.'

It's time to start living according to God's command and Christ's example, don't you think?

So the question is ours to answer – **When people see me, when people see you, what do they catch a glimpse of?**

Let's bring to the world a breath of fresh air.

Let's give those around us a glimpse of good living and of the living God.

3

Getting to Know More about Him

Love the
Lord your God
with all your heart,
soul, mind,
and strength.

Get to know Him.
You'll be glad you did.

The words I scribbled captured the moment that was going to change my heart and my forever. They were written on a scrap of paper during my first phone conversation with Steve Lindfors on July 18, 1989.

Our mutual friend, Mary, had arranged for the three of us to meet earlier in the week over lunch. There are two things I vividly remember about that 30-minute meal: Steve was a really nice guy. And I wanted to talk with him again.

Of course, I called Mary as soon as I got back to my office. She'd already talked to Steve, and he'd asked for my phone number. (*And the heavens opened, and glory filled my soul!*)

On the evening Steve said he'd call, I was ready. I sat on the couch in the very cramped one-bedroom apartment I shared with my sister, Lori. The big rotary-dial phone was placed on the floor right next to my feet, and I had paper and pencil ready to take notes. When the phone rang, I played it really cool. I just sat and stared at it for a couple moments, letting it ring, so I wouldn't seem too anxious. I was 32 years old, but I felt like a giddy junior high girl. (*Good grief!*)

Over the phone, Steve told me about himself. He said he had a deep interest in philosophy – existentialism and Kierkegaard in particular. (*I had no idea who or what he was talking about.*) He loved to read, and he was currently reading *The Russia House*. (*I went out and bought a copy that night.*) Baseball was his favorite sport, and he loved the Minnesota Twins. (*I knew my dad would like him!*) His family and faith were a significant part of his life. (*Whew!*)

More conversations followed. We got to know each other over the next few months. And love developed.

I'm so glad I didn't just sit and **think** about Steve after that first lunch, imagining who he was, creating a picture of him in my mind about what I thought he was like, assuming I knew what was important to him. That would have just been silly, right? Of course.

We start loving someone when we take the time to get to know them. We work at it. We share ideas. We ask questions. We listen. And in every relationship, love grows as we get to know more about them.

I've learned that the same thing happens in my God-and-Gaye relationship.

Consider this...

Jesus' friend and disciple, Mark, was part of the teaching moment when Jesus answered the question, "Of all the commandments, which is the most important?" Wow. Now that's a big deal question. Can't you just picture that scene? The whispering in the room stops, the people pause and lean forward, eyes focus on Jesus, wondering what this Teacher who has engaged them in such deep conversation is going to say.

The Teacher answers: **"The most important one ... Love the Lord your God with all your heart and with all your soul and with all your mind and with all your strength."**

The message couldn't be any clearer.

Jesus didn't rattle off rules. Doctrinal statements weren't stated. The lesson wasn't about doing.

The answer was about loving. It still is.

Loving God with every fiber of our being.

But ... How? How do we love God with every part of who we are?

The answer slips quickly into my soul. **We get to know Him.**

How do we do that?

– We read the letters He wrote to us.

– We talk with Him.

– We spend time with Him.

– We learn from others who also know Him.

– We nurture and cherish a relationship that is built on conversations, moments, prayers, tears, and celebrations.

Nothing has had a more significant impact on my life than getting to know God better.

The more I know Him, the more I trust Him. And when my trust increases, my faith increases. But it all begins with knowing Him.

A friend asked me the other day if I enjoyed listening to audio books. I said that I didn't. Holding a book with paper pages in my hands allows me to skim through some paragraphs when I'm bored, or tired, or not interested. I can be a good skimmer when I read. I don't want to be a good skimmer in my faith journey.

If there's one thing I want to avoid as I continue to get to know God better, it's skimming. I don't want to miss anything. I don't want my connection with Him to be superficial, only touching base on the main storyline. My commitment is all in or nothing. As we get to know each other, I may mess up, and I may argue with Him, but I never want to stop deepening our relationship.

I want to get to know God better. You too?

I want to love Him with every fiber of my being. You too?

Then, let's make sure we are spending time with Him, digging deep into what His heart is all about. Let's learn what it means to love Him with our whole heart, our soul, our mind, and our strength. No skimming.

God is the great lover of our souls. I also believe He loves philosophy, good books, baseball, conversations, family, and laughter. Things that matter to us.

That's so cool.

4

The Day I Lost a Day

We only get today once.
Let's not miss it.

several years ago, I lost Tuesday.

One moment I was doing burpees and lunges at the YMCA with my dear friend, Jody, and the next moment everything just got … lost. My last memory is of seeing myself walk into the locker room to get my gym bag. I remember tilting my head to the side as I stood in front of my locker, trying to get my bearings because the room was leaning sideways. The lockers looked like they were toppling over. But after that, nothing.

Steve and I later recreated those hours. At some point, I had called him. In between sobs I said, "I'm so confused. Something is wrong." He said he'd come and get me. I called him seven more times after that. When he pulled into the parking lot, I was standing outside the building, crying. I was a mess. I couldn't get my bearings. I didn't remember going to the Y and didn't know if I'd worked out.

Steve went inside and checked with the staff to see if I'd gotten hurt during my workout. He called Jody. Nothing had happened. Nothing explained how I had lost that time.

We went to the emergency room, and they took a bunch of blood tests and brain scans. At this point, I was "awake" but foggy, and thrilled that Steve was giving directions, telling me where to go and what to do. The doctors determined I had experienced an episode of transient global amnesia. Who knew there was such a thing! During that time, my brain was incapable of creating short-term memories. (*It's because I had no short-term memory that I kept calling Steve, even after I'd talked with him.*)

(*When the doctor told me that transient global amnesia was her diagnosis, I started to laugh. Because, really. Who gets amnesia when they're doing burpees at the Y? And if that's not a good enough reason to cancel all exercising, what is?)*

An overnight stay at the hospital allowed medical staff to watch for another episode and work at reducing my blood pressure. After a few days of a little rest and clearing out the fuzziness, I was good to go.

For the next few weeks, though, I couldn't stop thinking about how **I'd lost that time**. I still can't remember that afternoon. It was only a short few hours, but really, to lose control of your ability to see what's going on around you? Ooftah.

I'd had a similar experience a few years before that. Not nearly as traumatic or intense or scary, but just as odd. It was not my finest moment. It was worse than a bad moment.

I was working as the Corporate Employment Manager for a large firm in downtown Minneapolis. I interviewed people looking for jobs all day, finding the perfect fit between the candidates, and our needs, and I loved every minute of it.

But. One day…

I was interviewing a young man, and in the middle of the interview, **I woke up**.

Yes, that's right. I woke up. In the middle of the interview.

Somewhere between "Why are you interested in this position?" and "Tell me about a time when…" I fell asleep. Nevertheless, I kept asking the questions. I looked alert. Didn't seem to miss a beat.

I know the episode was only a few moments, but Oh. My. Word. The candidate had no idea I had taken a little nap while he was dazzling me with his skills and experience.

Good grief. I mean, really. GOOD GRIEF!

I don't know why it happened. I'm guessing it was a combination of a bad cold and lack of sleep and cough medicine. Clearly, I was not fully present for a few moments. The brain is a funny thing, isn't it?

That could-have-been-disastrous interview prompted me to really consider...

How many other times do I go through my day when I am not fully present, but I am fully awake?

You add my amnesia experience on top of that moment, and it's a question I still take very seriously.

Just think about this as it relates to really connecting and engaging with people. In any conversation, there are a gazillion opportunities to be distracted from the person we're talking with, someone who is right in front of us, right?

We see their lips moving and hear a few of the words they're saying – enough to nod our head and look interested at the appropriate times – but our minds are somewhere else. We're thinking about the work we still need to do. Or the groceries we need to pick up. Or how we don't really have time to be having the conversation.

(*Have mercy.*)

And how many times throughout our day have we just gone through the motions of living, without fully engaging, or being mindful, of what's going on around us? How much time are we missing by just **being unaware by choice**? Not just missing out on the little blessings that cross our paths, but missing out on the moments and people that we really care about?

"Teach us to number our days aright, that we may gain a heart of wisdom." This verse isn't about wondering how many days we have on this earth. It's about considering how we are living out the days that we are here, recognizing that we have no guarantees for tomorrow, or even for later today.

In his book, *Mastering Life Before It's Too Late: 10 Biblical Strategies for a Lifetime of Purpose,* Robert J. Morgan writes this:

> Lord, keep me from wasting time. Since You are infinite and my life on earth is brief, **teach me to count each day and to make each day count**. May I be a good steward of every moment. May I number my days like a miser counting his coins. When You look at my usage of time, may You see a heart of wisdom.

When we truly grasp how short life is, and how quickly it can change, we will **want** to make good choices that create a faithful and best life.

Here's what The Good Book has to say about this:

> So if you're serious about living this new resurrection life with Christ, act like it. Pursue the things over

which Christ presides. Don't shuffle along, eyes to the ground, absorbed with the things right in front of you. Look up, and be alert to what is going on around Christ – that's where the action is. See things from his perspective.

According to my doctor, we can't prevent an amnesia moment. But you and I both know we can prevent snoozing through life – we can stay alert when we are awake.

Let's not miss the moments, or the people, in front of us because we're shuffling along, looking at the ground, dozing. Whether it's the clerk in the check-out line who is clearly having a bad day, or the friend who is telling you her pains for the 73rd time, or the co-worker who insists on telling you how frustrated she is with her work … let's agree to be present. Right there in the moment. Not distracted by the activity around us. Not rushing through the conversation because we have something more important to do.

Let's capture the experiences each day offers – the colors, the emotions, the highs and lows. At the end of the day, let's know weariness **because we've given so much of ourselves into the moments and have enjoyed doing so**. We've laughed and studied and played and worked, fully alive.

Life is short, and life is good.

Let's not miss a moment of it.

5

Celebrating the Burpees!

You are **NOT TOO OLD** to live a fun, fulfilling life...

...To do 100 burpees? **PERHAPS.**

BUT **NOT** TO HAVE a really great life!

So, I decided to do a few burpees. Yeah, I know. I have no idea where that idea came from. If we've been friends for awhile, you know that I have this don't like / really don't like relationship with burpees. And if we're new friends (*Yeah!*), you'll figure this out quite quickly.

(Quick note: A burpee is an exercise form of torture. It requires you to jump and push and squat and do things with your body that, to my mind, the body really was not designed to do.)

For some reason known only to … well, I don't know who knows why … I feel compelled to do them at certain times in my life. (*Have mercy.*) Let's just say that it's not something on my when-I-want-to-have-fun-I-will-do-this list. Not ever. But inside the deepest corner in my brain, there is this notion that if I want to get healthier, I need to do burpees.

During one of my burpee moments, I wiggled and loosened up, stretched a bit, and got to it. A squat down, kick-my-feet-back, do a push-up, followed by a jump up with my arms reaching towards the sky. Then, I prayed my life wouldn't end, and that my elbows and knees and muscles would not give out. And then, I repeated. I did just enough burpees to count on one hand.

I finished the burpees and decided to focus on the fact that I had actually done them. Way to go me! High five! I'm an athlete! A little strut showed up in my step as I hobbled to the living room.

And then … I saw HER.

On Instagram.

The woman is an exercise expert. She posted a video of her burpee routine, which included LIFTING A WEIGHTED BALL OVER HER HEAD! I'm not kidding you. Who in the name of all things logical would ever do that?

The high-fives I had given myself earlier suddenly felt stupid. I mean, really – lifting a weighted ball over her head WHILE DOING BURPEES!

But ... Instead of adding Häagen Dazs ice cream to the grocery list and immediately running to Cub Foods, I chose to pause, and to think about what was messing with my heart and my mind.

My instinct was to feel less-than, and to feel sorry for myself. To have a standard that I couldn't meet flaunted in my face. Not good enough. I felt awkward and embarrassed about my imaginary high-fives. (*How silly is that?*)

But here's the deal. She is an expert. She's been doing burpees for years.

I travel in and out of the burpee world ... more out than in.

Oh, the experience is just like life, isn't it? Why do we think we must be good at everything? Just because someone else is smarter, faster, funnier, can do better and more burpees, better at fill-in-the-blank ... that does not give us a legitimate reason to downplay our own efforts and accomplishments.

One of my very favorite books is *Laughing Through the Ugly Cry and Finding Unstoppable Joy*, written by my friend, Dawn Barton. She has had a full package of life experiences and heartache, most of which we can't even imagine. Yet, she finds her way back to God in the middle of it all.

Dawn wrote about comparing herself to her seemingly perfect friend whom she called Tammi. Tammi is the friend who quickly causes you to feel frumpy and unskilled and just not enough. Not because of what she says or does, but because she can do so many things well. Nevertheless, here's what Dawn wrote about celebrating Tammi's gifts **and** our own gifts:

> We overlook our gifts because we believe they aren't as good as Tammi's gifts. Can you imagine if the great Andrea Bocelli stayed so fixated over his lack of eyesight that he chose not to sing? What if Julia Child was too sad to cook because she didn't have my flowing locks? Can you imagine a world without those scrumptious cookbooks just because Julia didn't feel her hair – or whatever physical feature – was good enough to be in the public eye? We all would have missed out on her talent.
>
> When I arrive at the gates of heaven, I will not have God look me in the eyes and say, 'Why didn't you use all of those glorious gifts I gave you?' I refuse to let my first words to our Lord and Savior be: 'Because I was worried that Tammi had better ones.'

As I write this book, I am in my 60s, and I'm *still* learning this important lesson … I am expected to be the "me" God has called me to be. You are expected to be the "you" God has called you to be. We are different from one another and that is a good thing. God has given you an individualized set of talents and characteristics and quirks and gifts that make you uniquely you. He's given me a different set. He has called each of us His child, and He has put each of us on this earth for a reason. For this time. **His desire is that we become who He created us to be.**

These words resonate, don't they? (*Take that, Burpee Queen!*)

We read this note of encouragement in Ephesians 2:10:

> For we are God's workmanship, created in Christ Jesus to do good works, which God prepared in advance for us to do.

If my four burpees were my best ... my high-fives were well deserved. Wearing the burpee crown will NEVER be my goal, and it will NEVER signal my success or significance. Why? I am a beautifully designed and intricately crafted piece of art – God's workmanship. **That's** what gives me my value. And burpees are not in my wheelhouse.

So, how about this ... Let's celebrate who God created us to be. Our uniqueness. Our talents. Let's celebrate all the times we give our best, regardless of what the scorecard says.

You bring your best to the world, and I'll bring my best.

You will shine, and I will shine.

And the world will be a better place because we both showed up.

6

Not in Charge

The joke is that Minnesota has two seasons – winter and road construction. Well, at the time I'm writing this, we've taken off our winter parkas, and the only way to get anywhere is to take a detour. We are well into road construction season.

There's a large highway overpass project just down the road from us. Exit ramps are blocked, and roads and ditches are filled with heavy equipment, taller than the trees. The massive trucks used to transport construction materials appear to have about 24 tires each, and these tires rumble when they move. Loudly. The mounds of dirt never seem to end, and cement trucks churn their loads night and day. Did I mention the detours? Around and around and around we go to bypass a quarter-mile of construction.

Driving by the construction site the other day, I said to my husband Steve, "I'm so glad I'm not in charge of that project."

A short time later, we wove around tar-carrying trucks, filling the formerly three-foot deep potholes that have turned into one large rut. And again, I said, "I'm so glad I'm not in charge of that project."

Ooftah!

As if!

I mean, really. There is nothing inside me that would remotely indicate that I should even consider getting to the place where I'd be in charge of those projects. I don't have those skills. Talent. Desire. Those are ducks I could never get in a row. You might as well ask me to run from here to Nebraska in four hours. This just won't happen.

And yet, somewhere deep inside a scary part of my brain, I'm celebrating that I'm not in charge of projects like mammoth road construction. As if there is an expectation that, of course, I would be involved simply because … because that's what I do! Fix things! (*Good grief.*)

Here's what I think…

When I'm faced with a problem, my instinct is to get involved. Solve the dilemma. Make it better. Control it. This is true especially when it comes to situations affecting people I care about. I want to fix the problem and make their pain go away instantly. So, I try. It doesn't matter if I'm capable of making it better or if I'm the best person to step in and help. No! I'm going to get something done now! And that creates an *Ooftah*! situation. Because oftentimes, I can't solve the problems. And I shouldn't.

Taking control of, and trying to fix situations that are clearly not something I should be in charge of, wears me out. And what my audacious assumption infers is, "I've got this, God. It's kind of a biggie. You can sit this one out." (*Really. How ridiculous and sad is that?*)

I think that when Matthew wrote his Gospel chapters in the Bible, he knew I'd one day be thinking about those big overpass projects and the aches in my friends' hearts. About how I would want to find solutions to help. And how that would make me very, very tired. So, he reminded me of what Jesus said:

> **Come to me**, all you who are weary and burdened, and I will give you rest. **Take my yoke upon you and learn from me**, for I am gentle and humble in

heart, and **you will find rest** for your souls. For my yoke is easy and my burden is light.

That sounds delightful, doesn't it?

I was getting worn out from the yoke I was wearing that involved pulling and struggling and being in charge and digging my heels in to manipulate situations to where I wanted them to go. Notice how Jesus describes what His invitation requires. I need to replace that yoke with the one Jesus extends to me – the yoke that will guide me to a place of peace, a yoke that will lead me to what He wants for me by showing me how He wants me to respond.

Oswald Chambers who wrote *My Utmost for His Highest,* is one of the smartest men of faith I know. Well, I don't really know him, but I've read some of his words, and I think that at least makes us acquaintances.

My friend Oswald responded to the words "I will give you rest·"

> Not – I will put you to bed and hold your hand and sing you to sleep; but – I will get you out of bed, out of the languor and exhaustion, out of the state of being half dead while you are alive; I will imbue you with the spirit of life, and you will be stayed by the perfection of vital activity.

Isn't that great news? I love his words," … the state of being half dead while you are alive … imbue you with the spirit of life … the perfection of vital activity."

There are three really important lessons here for you and me, my friend. First, we are not expected to be, nor should we be, the Chief Problem Solver for All Difficulties. Secondly, when God gives us rest from our own striving, He expects us to wake up and live! And third, when God sees a situation where we can be helpful, He will show us how to be helpful. Doesn't this realization make life feel easier?

There is very little I can do to help with a highway construction project. My role is simply to follow the detours and stay out of the way. But I know that there are times when I can help my friends. And my best help will be shaped by God's leading and direction.

I can surrender my cares and burden to Jesus. I can take his yoke and let Him guide me and give me rest, while He takes care of those problems in His divine way.

So then…

Thanks be to God that I am not in charge of the overpass or pothole projects.

Thanks be to God that I am not in charge of fixing anyone's problems.

Thanks be to God that I'm not in charge.

7

Like Playing Jazz

Listen to your neighbor's song.
Find her rhythm.
Lean in and engage.
Like playing jazz.

Good grief. I took them all so very seriously … piano competitions. (*You'd think that my entire life depended on playing Beethoven's "Moonlight Sonata" without making a mistake.*)

Months of practicing all boiled down to five minutes in a noiseless room that echoed when you pulled the piano bench over the wood floor. The "room of extreme nervousness" was empty except for a baby grand piano, an oblong table with judges, pencils raised, sitting behind it on folding chairs, and a few extra chairs in the back for anxious parents.

The competition. The judges. The nerves. The desire and deep need to play the song just perfectly. (*Have mercy.*)

I simply adore piano music, playing it and listening to it. The sounds that come from those black and white keys transport me to my Happy Place in a heartbeat. When I play, it's always about feeling the emotion – pulling life and energy from the keys. Knowing what notes to play, I have an ear for embellishing those notes – adding more emotion and extra keys. But playing piano always begins with the notes.

Not so with jazz.

I really wish I could play jazz piano.

In jazz, you let your soul lead, rather than the notes. You "feel the music," rather than "playing it right."

Watching Ramsey Lewis play jazz with his combo takes my heart and soul to a place that sings and tingles and smiles. When my favorite pianist is sitting at that keyboard, he becomes part of something bigger than himself, deeper than what he's feeling. His long fingers skim the ivories. His right leg bounces up and down as he picks up the rhythm, improvising as he responds to the other musicians. Glancing at the bass player, Ramsey flashes him a grin that says, "Oh, yeah. That sounded good." The musicians play with their eyes closed most of the time; written scores are not necessary. They are playing and responding to the music from their hearts, listening intently to each other while making amazing music.

"Like playing jazz" is how I want to love people.

It's so easy to expect everyone to live by the same rules, isn't it? By the written notes. By what someone has determined "right" and "wrong." Simplistic rules are formulated around issues that are complex, rules that prompt us to take sides, and rules we engage with defensively.

When rules are broken and notes are missed, we begin to believe that we aren't as good as we should be. That our neighbor – the other person – isn't as good as she should be. We count the wrong notes, rather than ignoring them and focusing instead on the music.

It's easier to live in a world where right notes are supposed to be played, where judges identify and call out the mistakes, because we believe we need to know who is right and who is wrong. We tell our neighbor, or friend, or a complete stranger, that her song is the wrong song. It's not a song we understand, so it must not be right. But. We are called to love. To listen to her song, find her rhythm, and listen to her music as a way of getting to know her. To lean in and engage.

We miss out on the absolute best music when we play as if we were in a command performance, requiring perfection and expecting the same from our neighbor, when we appreciate only the "right" notes.

And it is then, my friend, when we miss the connection. The combo. The music.

I'm learning to listen for the melody, and harmony, and syncopation in my neighbor's music, in all its glorious noise and messiness. I'm learning to listen to her heart.

I'm getting to know her.

Like playing jazz.

8

Little Prayers are OK

The God who hangs the stars knows your name. Wow.

The dentist's office is not my Happy Place. The place is not even in the same zip code. Or hemisphere. When the hygienist checks my blood pressure and tells me it's a little high, I try to act surprised. She doesn't know that my anxiety is about to make my head explode the minute they wrap that little napkin around my neck.

Once, I showed up with a big ol' cold sore on my upper lip. You can probably guess how comfortable that was when they stretched my mouth open, right?

This very sweet hygienist tried to get the "bite wing" X-rays taken of my mouth. Bless her. She just couldn't get the plastic thingy in place. I attempted to explain between tries that my mouth could not close because of that plastic thingy. Again, bless her.

I felt the tears coming (*The struggle is real, my friends.*), and I was wondering if I could just tell her this wasn't a good day for me to be at the dentist, and I'd reschedule.

But then...

I remembered what I'd read earlier that morning about prayer and remembered that I had committed to put my learnings into action, APPLY what I knew to be TRUTH. That meant I needed to pray.

So, I asked God to make the rest of the exam as easy and pain-free as possible, and to send my blood pressure into normal levels.

It seemed so silly to pray about a dentist appointment, but here's the deal...

Our little prayers are OK to pray.

Author and radio show host Susie Larson has written these helpful and encouraging words in her book on prayer:

> I pray like there's a God in heaven who hears me when I pray and who answers me when I call on Him. You know why? **Because there is a God in heaven who hears me when I pray and who answers me when I call on Him.**

Yes. Whether our prayers are for the little, or the big, God hears them. He is always leaning His ear towards us, listening ... then reaching out to answer us.

We know this is true because God says so. Check out what David writes in one of the Psalms:

> Is there anyplace I can go to avoid your Spirit? To be out of your sight? If I climb to the sky, you're there! If I go underground, you're there! If I flew on morning's wings to the far western horizon, you'd find me in a minute – you're already there waiting!

God knew what I was going through under that big lead blanket with the plastic thingy in my mouth, big plastic glasses over my eyes, and a big honkin' cold sore on my lip. So, I asked Him to turn the situation around and help me hold myself together.

And He did. He met me in my messiness. (*Why does that still surprise me sometimes? Good grief.*)

My friend, our prayers matter. Yes, it's important that we pray for the big deal things. And we are also taught,

> Do not be anxious about anything, but **in everything**, by prayer and petition, with thanksgiving, present your requests to God.

In everything.

That includes the visit to the dentist.

Thanks be to God.

9

Grasshoppers, Alzheimer's, and God

Shoveling grain is my least favorite job in the history of the whole world.

Standing in the back of dad's 2-ton red truck during grain harvest, shoveling the wheat down into the corners of the truck as fast as I could as it poured from our John Deere combine's auger was brutal. The temperature always seemed like it was 134° on those days. With no shade.

Did I mention the crickets? Those horrible little creatures joined the ugly old grasshoppers and took up considerable space in the back of that truck. And on me. They landed **everywhere**. No body part, or piece of clothing, was immune to their ickiness. (*Yes, "ickiness" is a real word.*)

The combination of choking grain dust, the intense heat, the miserable bugs, and the fact that I kept losing my balance in the shifting grain, made for a not-fun-at-all day.

But. That job created one of many experiences that taught me what it meant to work. To work hard. (*Can I hear an Amen! from my farmer friends?*) Learning to work hard was one of the best growing up lessons, and it was one of the most frustrating growing up lessons.

You see, because we learned to work hard, it was easy to believe that we **always** had to work hard, that we could **always** do it ourselves. But that principle doesn't work in every situation. Why not? Because there are some hard things in life that don't get better by working harder.

Alzheimer's is one of them. We saw that first-hand while caregiving for our mom. My sisters and I sure tried though.

We worked hard to help her keep her independence as long as she could. We worked hard to protect her sense of dignity. We worked hard to fill her apartment with joy and laughter. Most of those years, our hard work showed up in the **doing.** There were so many parts of her world that we could control, and we **did** the things to help her live well. It was a sacred, strenuous, laughter-filled, tear-filled, and beautiful season.

But the days came when her body got weaker. Her ability to communicate was more difficult. Physically caring for her was more challenging. Yet, we still worked hard. *"Come on, mom, just take one more sip." "Come on, mom, you can do this – just get up." "Here we go, mom, just move to your walker."* We tried so hard to get her back to what was, fearing what we knew what was going to be. Deep down we believed that if we stopped "helping" and if we stopped working hard, it would be our fault that she'd slip away faster.

But working harder was not going to work anymore.

You and I are so very fortunate that God gives us gifts and skills and opportunities to show up and make a difference for those whom we love so much, and for those God has called us to serve. We can run the errands. Go without sleep. Do the heavy lifting. Answer repetitive questions. Change our schedules. Ease their fears, and calm their hearts. We can do this work.

And there are times when we need to let go, even though everything inside us screams, *"If we just do this, it will be better." "We can't give up, it's too soon." "We've got to keep trying."* When that time comes, we need to take a really, really deep breath. Pause, and do the next, right, new thing.

Here's what I learned during that season with my mom. Although we had to let go of what we hoped could be, although we had to stop working hard on what we thought was best, **God didn't stop working hard.**

Let me tell you, friend. God showed up passionately. Fiercely. Lovingly. Compassionately. Divinely. He showed up in mom's final days, and in our grieving hearts. He didn't stop working hard on our behalf.

In those times when our hard work isn't working, He wants us to trust Him. He tells us it's OK to let go. We can stop fighting the battle on our own.

When the mountains loom large and we don't feel that we have the strength to move them, remember that it's our *faith* that moves them, not our hard work.

Paul reminds us of this in his letter to the Corinthians " … so that your faith might not rest on men's wisdom, but on God's power." I paraphrase that to read, "My faith cannot rest on my ability to make mom's life better or fix everyone's problems. My faith must rely on God's power."

I think what prevents us from giving up on our hard work is we are scared that God will intervene, but it won't be in the way we hope. Moms won't get better. Children will still suffer. Abuse, addiction, job loss, disease – they will still aggressively show up.

I wish I understood why God allows bad things to happen. But. The promise I cling to and know in the deepest part of my soul is that **God is faithful**. And everything that comes my way is wrapped in His love. Take a listen to Scott Krippayne's song, "*Sometimes He Calms the Storm.*" My favorite line, one I repeat over and over again when times are the toughest is "*Sometimes He calms the storm, and other times He calms His child.*"

My friend, your hard work may not be in caring for your mom. Your hard work might be your job situation ... a devastating loss ... dreams that have disappeared ... hurts that have sliced your heart in two.

If you are feeling a bit overwhelmed, worn out from working so very hard for so long, and you're tired of the situation you're trying to fix, or you wish would go way, stop struggling. Instead, sit down. Take a deep breath. Close your eyes. Whisper this to God ... "God, I'm tired. Will you please take this _____ (situation)? You are wise. You know best. Please move this mountain. You love us all so much. I give this to you. And as I'm waiting for you to do the moving and the heavy lifting, please give me peace."

For the last couple years, my sisters and I have set our phones to ring at 12:00 noon every day. It's time we've set aside for about a minute to specifically pray for our family. We each have our own prayer that we lift up to The One Who Loves Our Family So Much. For just a short moment, we pause, take a breath, and acknowledge that God is God, and we are not. We give Him our deepest cares and then, rest in His promises. Perhaps you'd like to do something like that too?

Paul writes again later in that chapter in Corinthians...

No eye has seen, no ear has heard, no mind has conceived what God has prepared for those who love him.

Now that brings hope.

So.

Sweet, weary friend, remember, you are not alone. Your heart cares deeply and loves ferociously. That is so good. And, God is right there next to you, wrapping His arm around you, swaying slightly like a mama comforts her baby. Listen to His voice. "I can take this. It's not too big for me. You can let go."

You can stop working so hard.

Let God see your hard task through.

Trust His perfect plan and perfect timing.

10

Cheese and Pickle Sandwiches

JESUS came to give us a FULL life. Not a 60% life.

John 10:10

Some days, life feels like a summer picnic. I'm enjoying a juicy cheeseburger (*grass-fed beef, done medium well, with a soft bun*), topped with ketchup and onion and relish, paired up with Ruffles chips, potato salad (*not too much mustard*), Bread & Butter pickles, and tangy baked beans. It's a day that brings all kinds of flavors, it's satisfying and refreshing. When the day ends, I sigh, "*Ahh. That was good.*" Everything feels right with the world.

On other days, it feels like the heavens have opened and life presented a made-to-order delight just for me. Bubbly Hawaiian pizza (*real cheese and Canadian bacon*) and gooey Special-K bars made with just the right amount of peanut butter and chocolate chips, served up with a glass of cold milk. The day that is exceptionally delicious.

And of course, there are those days that feel like a soggy paper plate covered with lutefisk and a side of pickled herring. How do I even describe this day? Stinky and sour.

However, most days, life is like a cheese and pickle sandwich. The day is a familiar kind of day. The cheese is mild, probably Cheddar, but the sweet and vinegary pickles deliver a little variety. Soft bread and soft butter. The ordinary is comfortable, but the routine isn't boring. There's a good taste and feel to it.

When our eyes open in that first squint in the morning, we really don't know what will happen in the next 24 hours. We may have plans and a schedule ... but heavenly days! We all know plans change, and schedules get up-ended, right? Who knows what the day is really going to bring?

Knowing that the day ahead will bring the known and unknown, I've made a commitment to myself. **No matter what is offered on today's menu, I am not going to miss it**. Every day is a delicious gift under a covered serving dish, waiting for me to lift the lid to see what's there. I want to experience the full meal in its entirety. Completely and intentionally engaged.

A familiar verse from Psalm 118 reminds us, "**This** is the day the Lord has made; let us rejoice and be glad in it."

The message is quite clear. God has given us this day, and this gives us reason for joy. Did you know, though, that when David wrote that Psalm, he was in a dark place and time? A few verses earlier we read these phrases:

> In my anguish I cried to the Lord, and he answered by setting me free ... they [enemies] surrounded me on every side ... they swarmed around me like bees ... I was pushed back and about to fall, but the Lord helped me.

Finding joy on pizza and Special-K bar days is easy. On the lutefisk and herring days? Not so much.

How we live each day – with gratitude, anger, or the blahs – is up to us. But every day brings opportunities for joy. Gladness. Celebration. How do we know this? The first verse of this Psalm, repeated as the last verse, tells us: "Give thanks to the Lord, for **he is good; his love endures forever.**"

Here's the deal.

(I wish I could hire a trio of trumpeters right now to slide up next to your reading chair and let loose a "Ta dah!" which

Dictionary.com defines as a "jovial interjection in making an announcement." 'Cuz this is an important announcement.)

When Jesus said He **"came so that they [we] may have life and have it in abundance," He was talking about a 100% abundant life**. Not a 65% life. Not an 80% life. And not a full life on just those days that serve the picnic lunch. A 100% life filled EVERY DAY with abundance … Including lutefisk and herring days.

Yes, there'll be days that "abundance" doesn't seem possible. But make those days the exception, not the rule. Yes, that pickled herring is going to show up sometimes, but it's not a meal that will last forever. Whatever the day offers, let's not miss it. Let's not fret about the annoying meals we had in our yesterdays, and let's not worry about what might show up on our plates in the future.

Let's be like Dorothy.

I met Dorothy at a women's retreat. She was wearing a beautiful cobalt blue blouse that brightened the whole room. Her eyes flashed and her whole face smiled as she *very enthusiastically* told me about her grandchildren. Did I mention that her hair was blue too? Delightful.

We giggled and connected about Jesus and hope, and I complimented her on her beautiful blue blouse. She said, *"Well, my hair color changed this month and I had to find something to match it. I usually mix different hair colors, but this month I ran out of all of them. So, I just mixed what was left of everything I had. Now my hair color changes every day! Today it's blue!"* And then she laughed. And shook her curly blue locks.

Dorothy's joy shone all weekend. She was a ray of sunshine and a barrel of fun. You could tell her joy came from a place *she's learned to go to find it.*

I want to be like Dorothy. She's watching for – and creating – great moments. **She's looking for the joy and giggles, not just waiting for them to show up. She turns her cheese and pickle sandwich days into a culinary feast.**

Let's enjoy today's menu. "Taste and see that **the Lord is good**; blessed is the man who takes refuge in him."

Life is short, and life is good.

Cheese and pickle sandwiches rock.

Let's live at 100% abundance.

(And perhaps make some radical changes to our hair color. Just because.)

11

Finding your Rhythm

Show yourself grace.
You'll find your new rhythm.

I t was a *"You've got to be kidding me!"* moment.

There were six of us, six middle-aged women who had dreamed of tap dancing on Broadway. But knowing that was never going to happen, we were exuberantly tapping on a grade school stage in St. Paul, Minnesota instead. After nine weeks of stumbling, sweating, and fighting shin splints, this was our big moment – our class recital. This was our chance to show friends and family how quickly our feet could move.

We had practiced. Hard. We had this.

We wore snappy purple coattails, purple top hats, purple cummerbunds, black leotards, and we swung jazzy canes. Very cool. (*You know this had to be a big deal to me if I was on a stage wearing tights and a body suit, right?*)

But, ooftah.

Ooftah happened at the final dress rehearsal, scheduled an hour before the live show. The 3-and-4-year-olds had just skipped off the stage in their pink tutus, and it was our turn to do our final run-through. We stood tall and proud, in formation, sucking in our stomachs, tipping our hats, canes angled to the side, with our front toes pointed perfectly towards the audience. The music cued, and we started tapping. *HOWEVER*, the tempo of the recorded music was very different from what we had practiced for MONTHS. KC & the Sunshine Band was singing *"Keep it Comin' Love"* in a tempo we'd never experienced, much faster than we had practiced. (*How does that even happen?*)

We could not get in sync with the music.

The music played, and we tapped **to the music in our heads** – the music we had practiced to – several beats behind what the sound system was playing. (*Muscle memory is a real thing, my friend. But we couldn't have tapped that fast if we wanted to*!) It would have been hysterically funny if we weren't so mortified.

No matter how hard we tried to keep up with the music, all six of us stayed in perfect sync with each other, but several beats behind the music.

Good grief.

That same out of sync feeling creeps up in different life moments, doesn't it? It sure does for me, even when I'm not wearing my cute little patent tap shoes with the black ribbons.

Children grow up. Jobs change. Relationships shift. Both good news and bad news influence how we move through life. We feel older as we try to navigate technology and all the "new" that vies for our attention. As life gets more complicated and noisier, and expectations increase, it's harder to find our rhythm. We feel "out of sorts." Getting our ducks in a row is out of the question – we can't even find the pond they're paddling in.

I think this is a time when we need to show ourselves and each other a little more Grace.

How about this...

When life's events invite some reflection, with a nod to something that needs to change, let's take the time to consider what's happening in our hearts. Appreciate what has been, and anticipate good things from what will be. When relationships change, let's celebrate what we had and celebrate what's ahead. When life gets hard and messy, and we can't keep up with everyone else who seems to be handling life well, let's stop the hurtful self-talk and appreciate the gifts and love we bring to our world.

Most importantly, let's keep looking up to the God who loves us so very deeply, who cares about our rhythm, and who walks with us every step, or tap, of the way.

The Bible is filled with stories of everyday people who were faced with circumstances that knocked them out of their rhythm at times. Two of my favorites are Moses and Joshua. Moses' story is filled with drama, miracles, sin, and holy restoration. (*The guy talked to God through a burning bush that was never consumed, so you know this is a must-read, right?*) He led the Israelites for 40 years. As the Israelites prepared to enter Canaan, the land God had promised to them, Moses transferred leadership to Joshua. What a life-changing event for Joshua! He now had the responsibility of leading two million people into a foreign land. There was so much he didn't know, and the task would certainly shift some long-standing relationships. But Joshua was known to be strong and brave and obedient.

When I get frustrated with technology I can't keep up with, or it seems as if I'm the only one who can't get my act together, I remember that the God who walked with Moses and Joshua is the same God who can take care of my iPhone as well as my heart.

The blessing Moses gave to Joshua is relevant and encouraging for our own shifts in responsibilities:

Be strong and courageous. Do not be afraid or terrified because of them, for the Lord your God goes with you; **he will never leave you nor forsake you**.

There's another verse that helps me find my equilibrium and get back in sync:

For the Lord God is a sun and shield; the Lord bestows favor and honor; **no good thing does he withhold from those whose walk is blameless**.

I pray that verse for friends, in my own words…

Lord, thank you for being the sun, her source of life, and protective shield for my friend. Give her the strength and courage, the favor, to do those things that she cannot do on her own. Develop her character so she remains respected and esteemed because others see you in her. Lord, please don't keep anything good from her life as she continues to walk with you. Amen.

We're going to miss the beat sometimes. It's OK to trip and miss a step. Just slow the tempo down a bit. Keep breathing deeply. Listen to the new rhythm. God will continue to lead and protect and give us just what we need to get back in sync. Eventually we will start to appreciate the new routine.

Back on the dance stage…

Our brave group of six couldn't catch up to the new tempo that afternoon. But we tapped our little hearts out in perfect rhythm with each other – confidently strutting our stuff, imagining Broadway lights.

Show yourself Grace.

You'll find your new rhythm.

12

Breathe. Just Breathe.

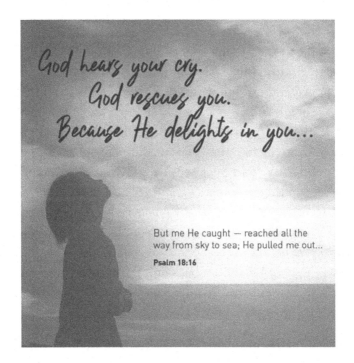

God hears your cry.
God rescues you.
Because He delights in you...

But me He caught — reached all the way from sky to sea; He pulled me out...

Psalm 18:16

I'm not much of a prime-time TV watcher. But I will never get tired of watching any show that has *NCIS* in its title. There are three shows in that media franchise right now, each one based in a different city. (*By the way, did you know that NCIS stands for Naval Criminal Investigative Service? Now you do! You're welcome.*) Anywhoo. Every time I watch one of the shows, Steve and I have the same conversation. My side of the conversation goes, "Yes, I know I've seen this episode 73 times. No, it does not matter."

Sam is one of the main characters in the *NCIS: LA* series. In one of the most startling episodes I've ever watched, his wife dies. Tragically. How? Carbon dioxide poisoning after being kidnapped and put into an unplugged portable freezer. She ran out of air, and eventually just stopped breathing. No air, no breath, no life. It was a scene that literally pulled me off the couch to my feet, and I watched it play out standing in front of the TV, with my hands over my mouth. I did not see that storyline coming. (*I know. It's a TV show. But it was an NCIS show. And they are my people.*) I kept repeating to the TV in a whisper … "No. No. No. No." Sam arrives too late to save her. He kneels next to her body, holds her close to his chest, and rocks her back and forth, softly repeating, "Breathe. Just breathe. Breathe. Just breathe." (*It was all a bit overwhelming for this die-hard fan.*)

You've probably heard me say this before: I believe that life is good. Really good.

And sometimes, life is more than an Ooftah. It's just plain exhausting. Taking another step forward requires too much – you just don't have it in you. Life is hard. Friends are struggling. And you're hanging on.

You just can't catch your breath.

We have all had those moments when everything feels tight. When our shallow breaths indicate we're doing everything we can just to hold it all together. What we really want is a good deep breath of fresh air, relaxed shoulder muscles, and a 10-hour nap. Something needs to change.

Author Leeana Tankersley understands these moments too:

> Sometimes a house feels tight, no matter how many square feet it is. Sometimes a heart and a life feel tight. Sometimes a marriage feels tight. Sometimes our work or our calling feel tight. Sometimes the skin we're in feels tight. We need a door or a window to open, a fresh breeze of perspective, the movement of change, but we don't always know how to get there from here.

We each have our own tight seasons. Maybe it's a time of caring for aging parents. Or worrying about people you love. Or a job situation that is draining every ounce of energy you have. Relationships within your own home that are strained and you are with those family members all the time. Have you discovered that the more you cling and worry and grasp, the more tense your body becomes, and the harder it is to breathe? Me too.

Dear sweet friend, you won't breathe easier until you pause and take a breath.

So, start there. Pause. Take a breath.

Psalm 18 is one of my very favorite Bible chapters. In it, we see such a powerful picture of God's love for us.

God hears your cry.

God rescues you.

God delights in you.

The Psalm writer, David, shares his experience with feeling restricted and tight:

> The ropes of death entangled me; floods of destruction swept over me. The grave wrapped its ropes around me; death laid a trap in my path.

Those ropes that were entangling him and wrapped around him would make it pretty difficult to breathe, right?

And then...

> I cried out to the Lord; yes, I prayed to my God for help. He heard me from his sanctuary; my cry to him reached his ears.

God heard David's desperate pleas, and with great force and intensity, **He rescued him**.

It's good to pay attention to **how** God shows up and rescues him. He does not respond like the driver of an underpowered automobile with a lawn mower engine and gas sputtering out of its tailpipe, held together with band-aids, limping along during freeway rush hour traffic, honking his horn, hoping the cars will slow down, opening his window and yelling out, "Excuse me! You – the big Dodge Ram 2500 over there – could you please move over?

I have a friend who needs me."

No!

Our God parts the heavens to get to us! He flies! He soars! Bolts of lightning and hailstones clear the way. Arrows scatter the enemies in front of him. He parts the water. And get this … the breath from his nostrils makes way! NOTHING will stop Him when we need to breathe.

And **why** does He do this? Why does He show up when He hears our cries? Because **He delights in us**.

Let me pause here and tell you…

I never, ever, ever want to go on a cruise. The thought of being stuck in the middle of a big body of water, knowing that it is possible for the ship to sink, takes me to a place of fear that is really almost silly. Drowning scares me. Not being able to breathe scares me. And falling overboard into the place where your feet can't touch anything firm – well, that combines drowning and not breathing. Not a good situation.

So, when David describes how God rescues us from the deep waters, I get almost giddy. I can feel the relief flowing through my entire body.

> He reached down from on high and took hold of me; **he drew me out of deep waters**. He rescued me from my powerful enemy, from my foes, who were too strong for me … He brought me out into a spacious place; he rescued me because he delighted in me.

For many years I have imagined "a spacious place" as a green meadow that goes as far as my eyes can see. Dancing in the long green grass are purple wildflowers, white daisies, and Black Eyed Susans. There's always a cool breeze, the sky is bright blue, and the sun shines on all of it. (*What I don't regularly share with others is that I see myself running barefoot through the field, wearing a cute blue and yellow mid-calf dress with a white ribbon tied in back, twirling around with outstretched arms like Maria in "The Sound of Music."*) No tightness, constrictions, or boundaries. And always … this is where I breathe deeply.

God sees that you're struggling for air. He hears your cries and will rescue you because He delights in you.

It's not God's plan for us to live tightly. I believe it grieves Him when we try to do the work that only He is capable of doing. He never intends for us to live among the overwhelmed, without peace.

So. For right now. Catch your breath. There is an immensely powerful, strong, loving, and caring God who is ready to meet you, an Almighty God who will draw you out of those waters.

Pause. Ask God to take hold of you and pull you into a spacious place.

And breathe. Just breathe.

13

Let It Go

Life can get messy.
And God meets us there.

Good heavens. We are so hard on ourselves, aren't we?

I was driving down Rice Street and noticed the white light blinking over the intersection ahead, indicating that an emergency vehicle was somewhere in the area. Checking my rear-view mirror, I saw the ambulance lights flashing, coming up fast behind me.

I pulled over to the side of the road, up against a curb. But there wasn't enough room on the shoulder to get completely out of the driving lane. The car behind me zipped around my Ford Fusion and pulled over in the next block where there was more space against the curb.

The ambulance swooshed by, blasting its horn as it did.

So, being the Midwestern, I-have-to-do-the-right-thing-always type of person, feeling guilty comes easily. Oldest child that I am, I started to feel guilty, because of the honking. I thought I'd done something wrong. I felt so awful that I hadn't gotten out of the ambulance's way fast enough. Or pulled over far enough. Or was even on the road. It didn't dawn on me until later that perhaps the paramedics were honking at the car that zoomed around me. Or they were preparing for the intersection ahead. Perhaps the honking wasn't even about me, right? But good grief. I assumed that the honking was directed at me as a scolding for breaking a rule, or doing something wrong, and I didn't know how to make it right.

I wanted to write a letter:

Dear Ambulance Driver, I am so sorry if I did something

wrong on Rice Street in front of you today. I don't know what it was, but I'm sorry. I didn't intend to do anything wrong. I don't know if I did anything wrong. And I am sorry if I did something wrong. Did I do something wrong? I'm sorry.

OK. Perhaps that exaggerates my thoughts a bit, but you get what I'm saying, right? If we think for even a moment that we have disappointed someone, said the wrong thing, not done enough, or made a mistake, we immediately need to do something about it. We don't even stop to consider if we are at fault, or have any responsibility in the situation. Even worse than perhaps being at fault, we imagine that the other person must think we are just a horrible human being for doing what we maybe did.

Good grief. Why do we even let our thinking go down that rabbit hole?

I think there are two beliefs that pop-up in moments like my ambulance situation:

> One. We think we should be above doing anything wrong … Ever.

> Two. We don't want people to think we did anything wrong … Ever.

Neither of those beliefs is based in truth.

There are a lot of pressures weighing on us these days. Why would we add to them by setting up our own unrealistic set of expectations that insist we can't make mistakes?

Let's just read that again, OK?…

…There are a lot of pressures weighing on us these days. Why would we add to them by setting up our own unrealistic set of expectations that insist we can't make mistakes?

The truth is that you and I **are** going to mess up, and at some point (*probably at a lot of points*), someone else is going to **think** we messed up. So. Let's just get rid of those expectations, shall we?

God never called us to a life of no messes. He does not expect perfection. And our belief that we can somehow convince people that we never mess up is just plain silly. This mindset comes from our own insecurities and self-absorption. (*Yeah, I know. Hard to think of it that way, isn't it?*) So, let's get over ourselves, shall we? We aren't that put together.

Paul, the great teacher and writer and one of the most important leaders in the early Christian movement tells it to us straight:

> This righteousness from God comes through faith in Jesus Christ to all who believe. There is no difference, **for all have sinned and fall short of the glory of God**, and are justified freely by his grace through the redemption that came by Christ Jesus.

Read those words again from *The Message* paraphrase, dear friend, and let the words sink in:

> Since we've compiled this long and sorry record as sinners (both us and them) and proved that **we are utterly incapable of living the glorious lives God wills for us**, God did it for us. Out of sheer

generosity he put us in right standing with himself. A pure gift. He got us out of the mess we're in and restored us to where he always wanted us to be. And he did it by means of Jesus Christ.

OK. Isn't that something?

Eugene H. Peterson, author of *The Message*, also wrote these life-breathing words:

Christ did not come to tell us how terrible we are but how forgiven we are.

The demeaning, less-than talk that passes through the zip code between my ears when I've messed up doesn't come from God's heart. My need to please everyone all the time and make sure no one thinks I would do anything wrong is just plain … stupid. Yes, stupid. Has anyone ever told you that people pleasing is a good thing, and you should make it one of your core values? No. Everybody knows this wrong thinking messes with us. Let's not do it, OK?

So, here's the deal. When we mess up, let's do what we need to do to make it right.

And for those times the horns honk, fingers point, and tongues wag, and we can't see that we're at fault, and we can't stand the thought that someone is thinking we did something wrong … take a breath. Let go of the guilt and remember the TRUTH. We **will** make mistakes. People **will** misunderstand us. It's OK.

God never called us to a life of no messes.

He never tells us how horrible we are.

Buckle up and live freely.

14

Something Wonderful is About to Happen

Always believe that something wonderful is about to happen.

My somewhat irregular morning exercise time is usually only a duration of 30 minutes, but by the way I carry-on, you'd think that I'd been sweating for 37 hours, with no break. I can't begin to count the number of times that I've flopped to the floor and dramatically whispered, through parched lips (*as if it's my last breath*), "I caaaaan't!"

I have forgotten … Exercising is a temporary event.

For all of 30 minutes, I believe I'm going to die on the bedroom carpet from sheer exhaustion, clad in a sweaty t-shirt, long shorts, and mismatched ankle socks. When the paramedics arrive, they will stand over me, shake their heads, and sigh. "It was the burpees. She should have known better. Poor thing."

I struggle with something similar when life gets tough for someone I care about.

Perhaps my response is because I'm the oldest child, or because I missed the "patience" gift when that characteristic was bestowed, or because my natural tendency is to make sure that all ducks stay beautifully and quietly in a row for my friend. Or maybe my response is because I forget that God is God and I am not. But when messiness arrives for someone I care about? I go into full **doing something** mode.

When someone in my life is struggling – all her ducks have abandoned the water, they can't find their sheltered habitats, and they are waddling down the middle of the highway – I get anxious and worried and wonder what I can do to make her situation better. (*Find the ducks now! Gather them together into the same pond! Nobody sleeps until they are back in a row!*) Fretting is my emotion of choice in those moments. Well, fretting and anxiety. And impatience. And weariness.

I begin to believe that the world will never be right again, that this sorrow, or disappointment, is moving in and taking up residence and sending the U-Haul away. That the world will never change. That this moment in all its frustration will define the rest of our lives. My concern for the person I care about runs deeeeep.

(*Good grief.*)

I have to remember that moments are … moments. Moments are not forever. Workouts and disappointments? They are … moments.

That really hard stuff that happens? It will eventually change. I'm not going to do burpees forever, the ducks won't stay on the highway forever, and God is going to take care of the person I'm caring about. The intensity of the moment is going to pass.

And yes, I know. Some of life's challenges stick around for the long haul. Bad things happen that have life-long consequences. But even during those seemingly never-ending seasons, there are moments when things are better, and life isn't so challenging. The intensity of the situation decreases, and we can relish those peaceful pauses. God never told us to live in a state of anxiety or fretting. He does not expect us to carry the weight of the world around on our shoulders. That's His job. And He can do it.

Think of all the **promises** we read in God's letters to us…

Why would you ever complain, O Jacob, or, whine, Israel, saying, 'God has lost track of me. He doesn't care what happens to me?' Don't you know anything? Haven't you been listening? God doesn't come and go. **God lasts**. He's Creator of all you can see or imagine. He doesn't get tired out, doesn't pause to catch his breath. And he knows everything, inside and out. He energizes those who get tired, gives fresh strength to dropouts. For even young people tire and drop out, young folk in their prime stumble and fall. But **those who wait upon God get fresh strength**. They spread their wings and soar like eagles, They run and don't get tired, they walk and don't lag behind.

You will keep in **perfect peace** all who trust in you, all whose thoughts are fixed on you!

And I am convinced that **nothing can ever separate us from God's love**. Neither death nor life, neither angels nor demons, neither our fears for today nor our worries about tomorrow – not even the powers of hell can separate us from God's love. No power in the sky above or in the earth below – indeed, nothing in all creation will ever be able to separate us from the love of God that is revealed in Christ Jesus our Lord.

(Could we have just a little sidebar moment here, friend? When I'm reading a book and the page has a few familiar Bible verses in it, I'm tempted to skim those verses, because they're familiar. But may I invite you to really read these verses here? You may find a new surprise that refreshes your faith in these divine words. I don't want you to miss God's encouragement.)

Look at the lilies of the field and how they
grow. They don't work or make their clothing,
yet Solomon in all his glory was not dressed
as beautifully as they are. And if God cares so
wonderfully for wildflowers that are here today and
thrown into the fire tomorrow, **he will certainly
care for you**.

Weeping may last through the night, but **joy comes
with the morning**.

I will never forget this awful time, as I grieve over
my loss. Yet I still dare to **hope** when I remember
this: **The faithful love of the Lord never ends! His
mercies never cease. Great is his faithfulness**; his
mercies begin afresh each morning.

The Bible is filled with examples and promises of God's
provision and perfect love. Not only does He carry us
through the messiness, He brings us good things as we
move through and out of our trials! Joy. Peace. Mercy. New
beginnings. Hope.

In the verses I've just mentioned, the two words that seem
to pull it all together are these:

God lasts.

That's **why** we can get through the tough moments, and
that's **how** we get through the tough moments. **And that's
why and how the people we care about will get through
the tough moments.**

Moments are moments. The tough ones will eventually turn
into not-so-tough-ones, even if they don't completely fade

away. And **in every single moment, God is there. Being God.**

Messy moments? They will come. Better moments? They will **most certainly** come.

Take a deep breath today.

Remember that God lasts.

Something wonderful is about to happen.

15

My Finguh Hurts

"It is wonderful what one ray of *sunshine* can do."

— Fyodor Dostoyevsky

He was a cute little guy with curly red hair, wearing a flannel shirt and little-boy jeans. He lay face down on the bottom platform of the Target shopping cart, dragging his chubby fingers along on the floor, singing a song he was composing in the moment as his mom moved through the produce section.

All was well with his world. Until…

One of those cute little fingers got pinched under a wheel of the cart.

He rolled off the bottom of the cart, jumped onto his feet, lifted his finger into the air while cradling his hand, crying at anyone who would listen … "My finguh! My finguh! I hurt my finguh!"

Big tears ran down his chubby cheeks, and the sobs bubbled up from his little tummy. He looked so frightened – not sure what he was supposed to do about his injury. He certainly wanted someone to realize this wasn't a good moment for him.

My first instinct was to run over and help him, look him in the eye, and tell him his finger would get better. But his mom was right there, so my attention didn't seem necessary.

But I wish I would have done so, because his mother just stood behind him, keeping her hands on the cart, not giving him a glance, and checking out the celery. "I told you not to drag your hands on the floor. That's what happens when you don't obey me."

The little guy just kept crying, shaking from his knees,

holding his finger in the air ... "My finguh! My finguh! I hurt my finguh!"

I'm telling you, friend, I started to cry right there in front of the carrots. That little guy's pain just tugged at my heart.

I was frustrated with his mom because I thought she should have responded differently. I wanted to somehow catch her attention and give her a look that would say, "Shouldn't you do something about this? Your boy is hurt. Do something." But I'm glad I paused and kept from showing my "tsk-tsk-tsk" expression. That wouldn't have been the loving response, and it would have been inappropriate.

I think my tears were for this little guy in his misery, *and* for the realization that there have been too many times when I have subtly, or not-so-subtly, expressed my disappointment because I thought someone had done the wrong thing.

Know what I mean?

(Oh, Lord, have mercy. For real. Please, have mercy.)

Sometimes, in my worst moments, I can be so quick to show my displeasure or give someone a signal that they have inconvenienced or disappointed me. For example:

– The clerk behind the check-out counter who is moving soooo slowly with her scanning. (*Deep exhale while looking at my watch.*)

– The customer service rep who finally picks up my call after I've been on hold for about 13 hours. (*Stern voice with direct expectations communicated.*)

– The restaurant server who has chosen to check his phone instead of bringing our order. (*Firm, repetitive finger taps on the table, accompanied with a looong glance in his direction.*)

My glances and finger taps and exhales aren't how I usually show-up. But even if it was just a few times, my signal of disappointment, or disapproval, had an effect on someone's day. That was a few times too many, and it's just wrong.

(*I need to say it again. Lord, have mercy.*)

My first response to "someone did something wrong" or "someone is not meeting my expectations" should be filled with Kindness. Compassion. Patience.

(*Oh, may I remember how Kindness can change the moment.*)

(*How Compassion can improve someone's day.*)

(*How Patience can hold the tears back, stop the tears, or dry the tears.*)

The Bible teaches us how to engage and respond to God's other children. The words aren't there for fluff. I need to remember that.

> The goal is to **bring out the best in others in the conversation**, not put them down, not cut them out.
>
> Therefore, as God's chosen people, holy and dearly loved, clothe yourselves with **compassion, kindness, humility, gentleness**, and **patience** … And over all these virtues **put on love**, which binds them all together in perfect unity.

(A little note here: "put on" requires us to take action. Love is a choice.)

Amy Carmichael, the missionary, hymn writer, and Jesus follower, has some direct and powerful words for us:

> If I belittle those whom I am called to serve, talk of their weak points in contrast perhaps with what I think of as my strong points … then I know nothing of Calvary love.

The clerks, the customer service reps, the restaurant servers, and the moms in the grocery store, are people with hearts whose lives may be much more challenging than we can imagine. Even if they disappoint us, **why wouldn't we show them patience and kindness and compassion when it costs us so little**?

Here's how I want to live…

When someone messes up and their "finguh" hurts, I'm going to drop the carrots, run over, look them in the eye, and make their boo-boo better. *And.* I'm going to give the mom a tender smile and encouraging look that says "I see you. Life is hard sometimes. You've got this."

I'm going to show up with Kindness. Compassion. Patience.

Join me?

You and me and Love.

We can change the world.

16

Kickin' Butt

Stay in the game.

God is faithful.

He's got you.

"**K**ickin' butt" doesn't seem like a lady-like phrase, does it? But when you use those words, people know exactly what you mean. (*Unless there's a meaning to these words that I don't know about, and they are too harsh, or very inappropriate for this book. Then, please forgive me for my ignorance.*)

My definition of "kickin' butt" – *Get out of my way because I'm getting things done and nothing is getting in my way.* Keeping with the title of this book – *Look out duckies! Paddle as if your lives depend on it, because you are getting in a row!*

When I write these little notes for you, someone might imagine that we are at a cozy coffee shop, drinking our grande vanilla tea lattes, sharing what's in our hearts and feeling all warm and affirmed. But realistically, we'd probably be at a pizza place, laughing out loud until we snorted.

Regardless of the location, let's just decide together that this is not one of those sweet and cozy moments, OK? Let's kick a little butt.

In honor of my deep love for football, let us imagine we're wearing the shoulder pads, helmet, mouth guard, quad pads, and the cleated shoes. We-are-in-the-game!

It's the 4th quarter, and the game is tied. Our team is exhausted, like the kind of exhaustion where you can't even stand up or see straight. The Gatorade jugs are empty, our muscles are on fire, and we have to go to the bathroom. We're on the sideline, checking in with the coach.

There are two ways this conversation could be going:

Option #1:

"Wow, coach. This has been quite the game, right? I've been out there almost every play. I've taken a lot of hits, and I think everything is black and blue. Pretty rough out there. Kind of wish we had a chiropractor on the sideline who could help me get my hips back in alignment because, well ... lots of hits today! You know, that other team is pretty big. I don't know if it's really safe to go back onto the field. I think I'm going to just take a rest here for a while. I've really put in my time. There are some other players that will probably show up and help bring this game home. Gonna' dash over to the concession stand and get a hot dog and coke and stand in front of that big fan on the sideline and watch the rest of the game."

Option #2:

"Wow. This has been quite the game, right? I've been out there almost every play. I've taken a lot of hits, and I think everything is black and blue. Pretty rough out there. But, man. Have we had some great plays! Everyone has stepped up and done exactly what they needed to do. What a great game. That other team sure is big, and they've made some great plays. But this game is far from over. We've got what it takes for the win, coach. Can I get back in now? Let's bring this home!"

I want to be the Option #2 Team Player who says, *"I'm still in the game."* You too?

I love to think that life is very similar to a football game (as long as we don't have to wear the tight pants). Life has worn out some of us. The battles have been too long, and we aren't seeing any rest in sight. It would be so much easier to coast. Let someone else pick up the slack. We're quite certain God has moved to another town and forgotten all about us.

But my friend, now is not the time to quit. God has not abandoned you. There is still reason to hope. God will give you everything you need to make the next play. You know, there are no verses and stories in the Bible that say it's OK to give up when times get tough, and life events and people seem too big and horrible. Change the game plan? Yes. Take a rest? Yes. Pause? Yes. Start again? Yes. But we don't quit.

I find great encouragement in knowing that I'm not the only one who sometimes wants to get off the field. People of faith since the very beginning have certainly faced much bigger obstacles with a lot more at stake than I have. They have taught me and encouraged me about how to keep going. Let's take a peek at how a few of them played when the game was on the line…

King Saul was anointed by God to lead Israel, but his disobedience, jealousy, and arrogance turned his life into a tragedy. His son, Jonathan, however, was a different story. He's the one I want on my team.

The Israelites were fighting one of their biggest rivalries, the big, tough, Philistines. (Note these stats: the Israelite army had 600 team members. The Philistine army had "three thousand chariots, six thousand charioteers, and soldiers as numerous as the sand on the seashore." Whoa! Not looking good for the home team!

Jonathan refused to quit fighting.

Jonathan said to his young armor-bearer, 'Come, let's go over to the outpost of those uncircumcised fellows. Perhaps the Lord will act in our behalf. Nothing can hinder the Lord from saving, whether by many or by few.'

The Message translation of the Bible says it this way: **"There's no rule that says God can only deliver by using a big army."** I love that thought!

And what was King Saul, the coach and team leader, doing while Jonathan came up with the new game plan? Saul was sitting under a pomegranate tree, probably fretting and wondering how they would ever get out of the mess.

Jonathan's courage and his trust in God resulted in a miraculous victory for the Israelites.

I want to play like Jonathan played. He believed in God's greatness, and he ignored the size of the battle. **He stayed in the game**.

A young Jewish girl named Esther was entered into the most intense beauty competition ever. A year of beauty treatments just to prepare to see if she would become Queen of Persia. Can you even imagine! A year just taking care of your looks! And she won.

Queen Esther learned of a plot designed to kill all the Jews – her people. She alone could prevent this mass murder. Knowing that appearing before the King and asking him to save their lives could get her killed, she still acted with courage. The King allowed her to come before him, and he granted her request to save the Jews. Lives were spared because one young woman knew that she may have been put in "royal position for such a time as this."

I want to play like Esther played. She understood what she was called to do, and she stepped out in courage despite the potential consequences. **She stayed in the game**.

And perhaps my favorite faith team – Shadrach, Meshach, and Abednego. King Nebuchadnezzar had built a 90-foot gold statue. Everyone in the kingdom was ordered to bow down to this idol. If they didn't, they would be thrown into a blazing furnace. Our three A-team players refused to worship the idol.

How did they respond?

> If you throw us in the fire, the God we serve can rescue us from your roaring furnace and anything else you might cook up, O king. But **even if he doesn't,** it wouldn't make a bit of difference, O king. We still wouldn't serve your gods or worship the gold statue you set up.

Even if not. No matter what game plan you throw at us, we will only bow to The One True God.

The three men of faith were thrown into the fiery furnace, and *they survived*. They were taken out of the flames alive and didn't even smell of smoke.

I want to play like these three played. They knew God could rescue them. And even if not---even if God allowed the king's evil plan to move forward – they knew it would be for their own good. They trusted God. **They stayed in the game.**

The players in each of these stories knew they were called to something bigger than themselves. They wanted to leave their mark in the name of the God they worshipped and loved so much. I want to do that, too.

Let's stay in the game.

And while we're listening to the play calls, let's remember this … **Our ability to stay in the game for the victory is completely dependent on who God says He is, not on how strong or capable we are**.

In my book, *God, Girlfriends & Chocolate*, I described how I believe God watches us play in our game of life…

> He is completely focused on our every decision, action, touchdown, and fumble. He cares for us, celebrates with us, and hurts with us. What a great image. Not only is God in the stands calling our names and cheering for us…
>
> He's calling our plays.
>
> He's running with us down the field.
>
> He's picking us up when we get hit hard.
>
> He's blocking for us when the big guys are driving.
>
> He's getting us back in the game when we drop the ball.
>
> He's giving us high-fives.

Need a little more pep rally encouragement? Tuck these power statements under your shoulder pads, and include them in your team meeting at half-time:

> Ah, Sovereign Lord, you have made the heavens and
> the earth by your great power and outstretched arm.
> **Nothing is too hard for you.**
>
> **Now to him who is able to do far more**
> **abundantly than all that we ask or think,**
> according to the power at work within us…
>
> Fear not, for **I am with you**; be not dismayed, for **I**
> **am your God; I will strengthen you, I will**
> **help you, I will uphold you** with my righteous
> right hand.

If we choose to look at how big the other players are, if we
choose to look at the enormity of our circumstances, if we
choose to believe the enemy is too big, we will call it quits.
Let's choose instead to look at how faithful our God is in
every situation, remember who is coaching us and calling
our plays, and believe that nothing and no one is bigger
than our Almighty God. Let's finish the game strong.

Do not quit.

Listen to The Coach.

The victory is promised to you.

Stay in the game.

Now. Go kick some butt.

17

The Rut Has to Go

You are
one choice away
from changing
your life.

A few years back I found myself in a rut. I'm not sure how I crawled into it. Perhaps, I took baby steps towards it over time with various habits and attitudes, and once I peeked into it, the rut just looked cozy. So, I snuggled in.

I'm going to assume that I'm not the only woman who has been a Rut-Resident, right? Here are some ways to know if we've hung the curtains, organized the pantry, and rut-settled.

We scroll through Instagram. Scroll through Facebook. Sometimes while eating ice cream. (*Often while eating ice cream.*)

We are simultaneously repulsed by and captivated by reality TV. (*Have mercy!*)

We dream of homey country kitchens and cute gadgets as we watch the cooking shows. (*Have you seen Master Chef Junior? Oh, my word. Those ahhhmazing kids can cook with food I've never even heard of!*)

We are watching others live their lives. Rut dwellers can build a club around this activity. We are observers. Intrigued with someone else's every day (*but sometimes not even close to the real world*) relationships and events. Even the really stupid shows or social media posts that make absolutely no sense command our attention. They are like a bad traffic accident – we can't look away.

Then, of course, our observations easily turn into comparisons. And unfortunately, what we see and read usually looks a lot more exciting than our own lives. The women we're watching all seemingly have their ducks in a row. Even when they claim they don't – pointing to their messy kitchens and messy hair buns and messy kids – their lives still seem more interesting than ours. Our daily "grind" feels same-old, same-old. Even boring. Less-than.

Sigh. We have become entrenched.

Did you know that ruts come in different shapes and sizes? Sometimes, it's what I just described – watching, wishing, and comparing. Sometimes, it's being too afraid to step out and do something new. And sometimes, we just need to change some aspect of our lives to get our spirits back.

When I caught myself buying new paint for the walls of my rut hut, I asked myself this question--***How do I get out of this?***

The solution was much simpler than I thought...

My rut-kicking began with a simple pair of sweatpants, those comfy pants that just make everything feel better. Of course, no sweatpants outfit is complete without the long t-shirt that covers everything you don't want to see, or remember. And if we're in the privacy of our own home? You know … bra not required, or expected. This is no fashion statement waiting to happen. We are just … comfortable.

But one morning, those sweatpants felt different. Or perhaps I should say, I felt different in them. I felt frumpy and wrinkled, which is different than comfortable, right? Feeling frumpy made me feel older. More tired. Really out of touch. Not a good rut to be in.

I decided I wanted to give up the "always feeling frumpy"

attitude. In a split second that morning, I decided that something needed to change. Now was the time to switch something up that would create a bit of energy in my world. I wanted to get back to **living my full life** and stop watching everybody else live theirs.

Do you remember the verse in the Bible where God says, "See, I am doing a new **thing**...?" Those words were my motivation.

I desperately needed a new thing.

So, I chose spandex capris – you know, the spandex that I should never, ever wear in public with a short crop top – the kind that holds everything in tight, and you actually feel like there is no more fat to jiggle. That kind of spandex capris. Yup. I found them in the back corner of my bottom drawer, and I put them on.

This is obviously not a big deal in the big scheme of life. And regarding "a new thing," I'm sure that the writer of that Bible verse never anticipated that His words would influence what I wear as my at-home attire.

But you know, swapping the sweats for capris made a difference. I felt more energetic in them. Less frumpy. More alive. It was a small change, but it signaled to my brain that there was "a new sheriff in town" and things were going to be different. Fewer pity parties, less boredom, and less self-absorption. More faith, increased fun, and a joy-filled attitude.

These days, decisions are not about whether I wear sweatpants or spandex capris. Decisions are about being intentional about how I want to live and feel. Tired? Frumpy? Thriving? Excited? Am I doing the things that breathe life into me and bring me joy?

I'm not crawling back into the rut.

What's your rut, Buttercup? Feeling like it's time to make a break for it? Whether you're in a rut with your job, your routine, your clothes, your attitude ... whatever your rut looks like, you can choose to leave it like I have. You can try something new. **Let God do a new thing in your life**.

Start again. Make a change, and find your own capris.

I'm high-fiving you all the way!

18

Life Whisperers

Who are your
life
whisperers?

It matters.

I've been talking to screens – TV, iPad, and iPhone screens.

Good grief.

My messages are usually in response to politicians who are talking intensely at me, telling me what to believe, or social media engagers who are informing me that my thinking is right or wrong, or good or bad.

It all just gets to be too much, doesn't it? Sometimes, my responses to the screens get a little ... well, let's just say I'm tired of the noise. The words and tones of the rabble rousers give me a headache.

My husband Steve and I were watching a MASTERPIECE TV show on our local PBS station the other evening. The characters had these delightful British accents, and I found myself wanting to speak "in British" as I watched. Because it seemed so cool. "Hey, hey Steve. Fancy a cuppa tea, would you?"

Several of my friends have fabulous Texas drawls and use phrases that sound as smooth as butter. You know, where every sentence includes a "Y'all" and is filled with charming sweetness. "Aww. Bless your heart." When I'm alone at home, I'll sometimes pretend I'm from the South, which gives me permission to speak like them. I feel so ... sweet and smooth.

And of course. You put me in any conversation with someone from Norway, or someone who speaks Norwegian, and I'm desperate to speak like them. "Du er så snill," is said with a sing-songy kind of voice. (*You are so kind.*) The sentence can fit into almost any conversation. My heart swells with joy for the opportunity to sound like I can speak the heavenly language. Memories take me back years to our hometown cafe. None of the local farmers came from Norway, but when they gathered there for their morning coffee, they all sounded like they just got off the boat.

Friend, who you listen to matters. How they speak to you matters. Because their words and their tone influence your mind and spirit.

You and I need to be very intentional about who has access to our ears, don't we? Whomever has access to our ears has access to our hearts and our minds, which has a profound impact on how we think. How we think has a profound influence on how we live our lives.

Do you remember the Bible story about the 12 men Moses sent to scope out the land of Caanan? God had promised to give the Israelites this land. It was the Promised Land. It was theirs. The Israelites had traveled out of Egypt and were ready to settle into their new home. But Moses wanted this team of 12 to check things out first. What is the soil like? What about their crops? What do the people look like? How big and how fortified are their cities? He wanted to know about the land so they could prepare the best strategy for moving into it.

Sounds like strong leadership and good planning to me. The advance team of 12 set out on their 40-day recon mission. But things started to fall apart when the team returned with their report.

All 12 scouts agreed that the land was filled with milk and

honey. The produce was impressive – it took two men to carry a pole with one cluster of grapes hanging from it.

But...

Ten of the 12 let fear control them and influence what they reported and how they reported it.

> But the people who live there are powerful, and the cities are fortified and very large. We even saw descendants of Anak there.

The other two scouts, Caleb and Joshua, disagreed.

> We should go up and take possession of the land, for we can certainly do it.

(Musical interlude here. Re-reading this story makes me start humming an old Sunday School song. You, too?)

> *Twelve men went to spy on Canaan*
>
> *Ten saw bad and two saw good*
>
> *What did they see when they spied on Canaan?*
>
> *Ten saw bad and two saw good*
>
> *Some saw giants big and tall*
>
> *Some saw grapes so big they fall*
>
> *Some saw God was in it all*
>
> *Ten saw bad and two saw good*

Now. Back to our regularly scheduled story...

The ten men strengthened their doom and gloom report.

> They spread among the Israelites a bad report about the land they had explored. They said, 'The land we explored devours those living in it. All the people we saw there are of great size ... We seemed like grasshoppers in our own eyes, and we looked the same to them.'

In order to confirm their fears, the ten embellished their report to make the circumstances sound even worse. They focused on the situation in front of them. Joshua and Caleb focused on God's promise.

The Israelites listened to the ten who had no faith. And then they wanted to overthrow Moses, stone Joshua and Caleb, and actually wished they were back in Egypt. They didn't take responsibility for their critical thinking failure or their own lack of faith. They blamed their despair on those voices (a/k/a politicians, angry friends, social media posts, etc.). "Where can we go? **Our brothers have made us lose heart**."

The distance between Egypt and Canaan was only 150 miles. The Israelites could have enjoyed the land of milk and honey after traveling another month or so. Instead, they spent 40 years wandering in the wilderness. The entire generation of men who left Egypt died in the desert during their wanderings. Only Joshua and Caleb from that generation – two out of two million – were allowed to enter this Promised Land.

The people listened to the wrong voices.

Who are we allowing to speak into our souls and minds? Is God on our short list? If we are listening to the angry, the contentious, the distortions, and the fear, we won't be able to discern God's voice. And no voice is more important to hear.

I introduced you to my friend, Oswald, in an earlier story. (a/k/a Oswald Chambers, the great evangelist and teacher.) Here is another message from this wise man:

> Is my ear so keen to hear the tiniest whisper of the Spirit that I know what I should do? ... He does not come with a voice like thunder; His voice is so gentle that it is easy to ignore it. **The one thing that keeps the conscience sensitive to Him is the continual habit of being open to God on the inside.**

God desires to speak with us. Connect with us. Teach us. Encourage us.

> Your own ears will hear him. Right behind you a voice will say, 'This is the way you should go,' whether to the right or to the left.

> My sheep listen to my voice; I know them, and they follow me.

If we aren't listening for Him, we'll miss his voice. And that is tragic.

Who are we listening to? What are we reading? Watching?

News? Social media? People/friends who are not living joy-filled lives?

Words of hope from The Good Book? Pastors and teachers

who remind us of God's promises? Faithful friends who speak truth into our lives?

Are we hearing God's voice?

Perhaps if God's voice seems dim and lost in the noise of the louder voices, it's not because He's not speaking. It's because we aren't listening. We need to pause. Be still. Earnestly say as the prophet Samuel did, "Speak, Lord, for your servant is listening." And then listen.

Who are your life whisperers? Who are you listening to first? Have you made room for God's voice?

I'm choosing to listen first and most intently for the voice of The One Who Loves Me Most. Then I welcome messages from faith-filled and joy-filled voices, trusted voices who lovingly challenge and encourage me, voices that bring a breath of fresh air and refresh my soul. And of course, British accents, Southern sweet drawls, and Norwegian lilts are music to my ears!

Speak, Lord, for your servant is listening.

19

When the Parade Passes By

Life is a parade!
Let's not miss it!

What is it about parades?

They prompt us to spontaneously cheer and clap. Wave at people we don't know. Bounce to the music. Hope that fistfuls of candy gets thrown our way. And many of us get misty with nostalgia as the high school bands pass by. At what other event do we act like this?

The "professional" parades on television are OK to watch, right? Macy's Thanksgiving Parade invites our ooh's and aah's from the comfort of our couches, while encouraging our inner parade critic. We select the floats we like best, worry the girls carrying the flags will freeze to death, and wonder who has the money to pay for all of the spectacle.

BUT!

The really cool parades are the ones that walk down our main streets – those with people we know sitting in the back seat of a convertible with the sign that says "Dairy Princess" – a pick-up carrying the "Class of 1975" in its backend – floats built on flatbed trailers with massive amounts of bright paper mache flowers stapled to their frames – dozens of kids riding bikes and trikes decorated with colorful streamers as their parents walk along the perimeter taking videos and carrying water bottles – the fire engine spraying water that cools everybody down – the old-time John Deere tractor, sputtering along with its smoking chimney, followed by the new and massive John Deere machine strutting its stuff – and finally, the hometown marching band, filled with musicians struggling to walk to the beat because, well, have you tried to walk in a straight line and play a clarinet as your music blows around in 93° weather? (*And yet, we think it's the best they've ever sounded!*)

We don't ooh-and-aah because the parade is fancy, or because the floats are perfectly designed, or because everyone marches in military precision. We ooh-and-aah because we're celebrating our friends. We're cheering for the floats and pick-ups and flatbed trucks that carry people we know and love. We clap for the memories and the community the event represents. We smile and laugh because we see the beauty in the people. The moments. The joy.

That's my kind of parade.

I saw a different parade scene in a photo on social media recently.

The picture captured a large group of parade-watchers crowded onto a sidewalk. Too many people in too little space. The scene highlighted an elderly woman calmly resting her arms on the street barrier, leaning into the parade action. Smiling. Soaking it all in. Feeling the energy. Not missing a thing. She was the only person watching the parade.

The people standing around this contented woman were focused on taking selfies. Posing. Finding the right light. Looking at their phone cameras with their backs to the street. Missing the parade. Missing out on the experience.

Now, I sure don't mind selfies. I'm glad someone thought of a way to put us into a memory moment without our requiring a tripod and a photographer.

However, whether it's a parade, or it's my life, I want to capture the experience, not just the selfie. Lean into what's in front of me and watch the details play out. Feel the emotions that coincide with the event. Focus on being fully present in that moment. Not worry about the lighting or the best angle.

What if we looked at every day as a parade to lean into and celebrate?

There's good stuff happening around us, right in front of us, every day, situations to cheer for and clap for and ooh-and-aah over. Sometimes it's the unexpected text or email from that friend who knows just what to say, or a giggle from the little buddy in the stroller – the helpful clerk in the store who knows where to find the chia seeds – the subtle Midwest greeting we use when we're driving … raise just your pointer finger while keeping the rest of your fingers wrapped around the steering wheel of the pickup.

"Good stuff" is the colorful flower bed after a fresh rain – the hot summer days with beach towels and the smell of sunscreen – donuts on Friday – NCIS TV reruns – twilight when the weather is cooler and only the toads and crickets and mourning doves are talking among themselves.

Life is a parade of beautiful moments, people, and events.

Let's look for those daily flashes of brightness that bring joy, gratitude, and giggles. And then lean into them. Not always rushing to the next thing. Taking time – even just seconds – to live in that moment. Doesn't this sound like a great plan? I think so, too.

Let's stop the rushing.

Let's appreciate what's in front of us.

Let's watch the parade.

> *"**This** is the day the Lord has made;*
> *let us rejoice and be glad in it."*

20

Grace, Mercy, Love, and Dignity

I was walking past the graham crackers in the grocery store when an elderly woman wrapped in a blue wool coat and pushing a grocery cart, rushed up to me.

"Where are the paper towels?"

Her sense of urgency immediately caught my attention. It came through her voice and her eyes. Panic. Anxiety. Lots of it.

"My husband had an 'accident.' He's sitting in the car, he's so embarrassed. We're on our way to a quartet reunion, and they're waiting for us."

(*Oh my. Can't you imagine all the emotions her trembling heart was experiencing in those moments?*) I just wanted to hug her and make everything better. But there wasn't time for hugging. We needed supplies. I grabbed her hand and the cart. "Follow me!"

Two aisles over, I pointed her in the direction of the baby wipes while I dashed to get baggies and paper towels. We quickly gathered what she needed, and then she stopped and looked at me. She gave me a hug. While her tears came, she whispered, "Aren't Minnesota people just the best? So willing to be helpful and kind."

And then she scuttled to the check-out lane.

And I stood in front of the paper towels and cried.

For hours after that, I seriously thought about ... dignity. What is the experience like when you want dignity, but circumstances bump up against it?

I think it's easy for us to consider a person's dignity when we encounter the elderly. Or someone who needs significant help. Or someone more vulnerable. But you know? (*I think you do* …) Dignity is something every single one of us looks for, even when we've messed up. Especially when we've messed up.

In our work cubicles. In the restaurants. In the check-out lines. In the church pews. The customer service rep on the other end of the line who does not seem helpful. Someone we love who disappoints us and stinging words seem like the appropriate response.

Dignity. We fight for it within ourselves. All. The. Time.

We want to interact with someone who helps us hold our head up, rather than forcing us to lower it in shame.

We want to be around someone who listens with their heart, rather than blowing us off.

The gift of dignity is given so graciously by Jesus. Read these words with a fresh set of eyes, as if you were watching the scene play out on a big screen…

> At dawn he [Jesus] appeared again in the temple courts, where all the people gathered around him, and he sat down to teach them. The teachers of the law and the Pharisees brought in a woman caught in adultery. They made her stand before the group and said to Jesus, 'Teacher, this woman was caught in the act of adultery. In the Law Moses commanded us to stone such women. Now what do you say?' They were using this question as a trap, in order to have

a basis for accusing him. But Jesus bent down and started to write on the ground with his finger. When they kept on questioning him, he straightened up and said to them, 'If any one of you is without sin, let him be the first to throw a stone at her.' Again he stooped down and wrote on the ground. At this, those who heard began to go away one at a time, the older ones first, until only Jesus was left, with the woman still standing there. Jesus straightened up and asked her, 'Woman, where are they? Has no one condemned you?' 'No one, sir,' she said. 'Then neither do I condemn you,' Jesus declared. 'Go now and leave your life of sin.'

(Maybe, like me, you just want to pause here for a moment to think about what this woman was experiencing. So little dignity, and so much dignity restored. Such callous nastiness and so much love offered.)

The story tells us that there were a lot of people at the temple. Watching. And then the "Important people" came hustling in. Can't you picture them pushing people out of the way, pulling or dragging this poor woman with them? Can you imagine the tears that must have been streaming down her face while she begged them to stop? Then, they forced her to stand in front of all of them as they shamed her and shared what was probably her deepest secret – her adultery. They were manipulating her hurt and messiness for their own advantage. And her humiliation. Embarrassment.

Notice how Jesus didn't react to the Pharisees' anger. He didn't scold them for their hypocrisy. He didn't take on their posture of anger and self-righteousness. He made his point with one statement, and they slithered away to lay their traps for another day.

I imagine the woman was trembling when Jesus spoke to her, realizing her life had just been spared, but knowing that Jesus knew all about her sin. What did Jesus do? He met her first with love, grace, and mercy. And then he told her to quit sinning. Love, grace, and mercy first. To restore her dignity.

This woman probably left the temple courts completely wiped out by the trauma. I'm sure there were people standing on the fringes whispering and pointing and shaking their heads. But don't you think her heart felt a little lighter? That she may have lifted her head up a bit? Don't you believe she would choose to sin no more? She had experienced grace and mercy and forgiveness and love in a very real way. Her dignity had been restored.

Jesus had given that woman a chance to pause and take a breath. And then she began her new life.

Yes, it's up to us to help someone like the woman in the blue wool coat in the grocery store keep their dignity when life has thrown a curveball. It's also up to us to help someone find, or keep, their dignity when they have really messed up their lives by making bad choices. Isn't that what love is all about?

Jesus taught us the greatest commandment:

> **Love the Lord your God with all your heart and with all your soul and with all your mind. This is the first and greatest commandment. And the second is like it: 'Love your neighbor as yourself.'**

Let's not miss one single opportunity to remind someone that their life is valuable. And when the opportunity arises, **let's lead with grace and mercy and love**. Let's leave them with some dignity.

Who around you might be feeling a little less-than today? Be aware and watch for that moment.

Then, share a good word. Bring on the encouragement. Make a real difference.

Grace. Mercy. Love.

That's where we start.

Dignity.

It matters.

21

Finish the Race

Don't quit.
Finish the race.

There are moments that cannot be erased from my memory bank. My eyes can't un-see what I saw, and my muscles can't forget what I endured.

Stroll with me back to Physical Education class in the 1970s. Climax School gymnasium.

We had to wear a one-piece, navy-blue gym uniform with elastic around the waist, elastic around the arms, elastic around the thighs, and snaps up the front. (*Really? Are you serious?*) Did the designer have any clue about what your stomach and butt look like when you wear such a thing? Absolutely nothing attractive or flattering about this piece of clothing!

As if that wasn't humiliating enough, we had to exercise to the music of ... wait for it ... the *"Chicken Fat"* song. (*Have mercy!*) The song was President John F. Kennedy's brainchild to inspire us to get in shape. It was designed to "give that chicken fat back to the chicken" by moving us through a series of floor exercises. The lyrics that are seared into many of our middle-aged memories: "Go, you chicken fat, go away! Go, you chicken fat, go!"

Who in the name of all things healthy and fashionable ever thought that was a good idea? Michelin Man-looking uniforms and a chicken fat tune?

(*Good grief.*)

So, we had the very stylish one-piece elasticized jump suit, and bouncy music to get us motivated. That brings us to ... The Presidential Fitness Test.

Remember that? Every spring we'd have to go through a

fitness assessment that included an obstacle course (*Anyone besides me hate to crawl on your belly with your butt in the air?*), a rope climb (*We had never, ever climbed a rope.*), jumping the hurdles (*ouch, ouch, ouch*), and ... running. That was the worst. The running.

In the little town I grew up in, we would run around the bus track behind the school. I don't remember how many times we circled that gravel road, but I do remember how painful the whole experience was.

After the first ... oh, several hundred feet ... my knees and thighs would start to smart, and I'd get a little winded. The longer I ran, the more my legs hurt. Then, my lungs would start to burn. And of course, the more they hurt and burned, the more I focused on the pain. You get this, right? (*Oh, my poor knee ... I think my lungs are going to explode ... this hurts too much ... I think my leg is falling off ... I wonder if anyone would care if I just laid down on this horrible gravel road and died right here.*)

Yes, running was hard work.

But the toughest workout was taking place between my ears, in my mind – my thinking.

The more I focused on how tired I was, the ache in my knee, and the fire burning in my lungs, the harder the run became. I just wanted to quit.

That describes some moments in my life.

(*Aha, yes. Who knew that wearing a navy-blue uniform while listening to the "Chicken Fat" song and then running around a bus track until I thought I was going to die would result in a transformational moment as an adult. But here we are.*)

It's like this...

I'm caught up in a frustration, or mini-crisis, or a tough situation, and all I can think about is how hard it is to function. How nothing looks or feels right. My focus is on my exhaustion, frustration, and aches and pains. Nothing exists except the you've-got-to-be-kidding me scenario. Do you know what I'm talking about? I figured you would.

And yet.

I know, I know, I know, that if I would just pause and stop the negative spiral I'm in, things could look and feel a little better. It's so easy to get all tangled up in the messiness, isn't it? If I would just stop and catch my breath, I could change my perspective. My brain would be better able to consider new solutions or form a more appropriate response. Life would be easier. And I'd finish the race.

I need to stop and take a breath. And then start again.

This life you and I are living isn't intended to be a sprint. It is a long run that requires water stops. Naps. Recalculating our route when we get off track. Letting go of the things (people, activities, priorities, and commitments) that keep us from being who God has called us to be.

God wants us to finish our race – our life – living it fully and joyfully!

> Therefore, since we are surrounded by such a great cloud of witnesses, let us throw off everything that hinders and the sin that so easily entangles. And **let us run with perseverance the race marked out for us.**

I love the words used in *The Message* translation of that same verse:

> Do you see what this means – all these pioneers who blazed the way, all these veterans cheering us on? It means we'd better get on with it. **Strip down, start running – and never quit!** No extra spiritual fat, no parasitic sins. **Keep your eyes on Jesus**, who both began and finished this race we're in.

Pause. Get rid of the stuff that weighs us down, stuff like unbelief. Lies masqueraded as truths. Sin that trips us up. Anything that takes our eyes off Jesus. Then, take a breath. And start again. **Finish the race.**

This is such a wonderful verse. I love that God understands we can get sidetracked. I love that He encourages us to persevere and keep going.

And let's not miss this. Did you notice the bonus message in that verse of encouragement? Did you catch it?

All of heaven is cheering us on! How cool is that? Every race and every racer needs the excitement that comes from people in the bleachers, or standing alongside the road jumping up and down, waving their posters, and screaming from their bellies for those runners brave enough to run around in shorts.

We've got our own pep club! I can just see those saints who've gone before us, peering through the clouds, leaning over the sunbeams, elbowing each other to get a good view, shouting and encouraging us … "Look at her go! You've got this! Keep going! Don't stop now! You're doing great!"

Oh, **life is good and God is faithful.** And the race is ours to finish.

My friend, whether we walk or run … let's keep going. Let's not quit.

When our knees and lungs and hearts and souls start to hurt, let's remember to pause. Take a breath, and then, start again. We can do this.

Finish the race.

All of heaven is cheering us on.

WOW.

22

Getting My Ducks in a Row. Or Not.

> I DON'T HAVE ALL, NOT EVEN SOME, OF MY DUCKS IN A ROW...
>
> BUT THEY ARE ALL IN THE SAME POND, SO I HAVE THAT GOING FOR ME...WHICH IS COOL.

Image used with permission from Kim Garst's Social Content Club:
https://kimgarst.com/courses/gosocial-content-club

H ere's what I've learned.

It is very difficult to get my ducks in a row.

And I get really tired trying.

You know what else I've learned?

God doesn't require me to get my ducks in a row before He will use me.

He can use me even while I'm **looking** for my ducks.

How many times have I muttered under my breath, "*I just need to get my act together.*" "*I gotta' get my ducks in a row.*"? When those whispers come, my life is spinning, and I can't get a grip on my priorities and schedule. Defeat and chaos are my constant companions. You know what I mean, right? The ducks I'm trying to gather aren't even in the same pond!

Perhaps you've discovered through my stories that I have struggled with a few of my little duckies over the years. I even named the ones I nurtured and tended to – "Fret." "Tension." "Strive." For reasons that I believed were noble and right, I worked hard to fix situations, rather than giving up control. I worried about disappointing people, rather than focusing on how to love them. And in my attempts to get all the details in perfect order, I missed some moments. Those ducks were paddling so fast under water that they just kept going in circles.

Ooftah.

My roommate in Bible school was a powerful woman of prayer. She would go into the tiny closet in our dorm room in the morning, and I would hear her pour her heart out to God, praying with tears about things that mattered. I would go into that same closet and get distracted by all the dust bunnies.

During my early years of walking with God, I would get both encouraged and discouraged when I'd look at the stories of great women of faith. When I saw what God was doing through women who said YES to His leading, something would stir deeply inside me. I wanted to be used by God too. But then I would start to compare my journey with theirs. Mine seemed so uneventful and less-than. I believed that I had to have very intense emotions, great spiritual disciplines, and be a Biblical scholar – that I really had to have my act together before He'd be able to use me.

I was wrong.

I would soon learn that God is God, and I am not. I serve Him because of **His** strength, not because of my abilities. It is OK that my ducks aren't always interested in getting into a row. God can handle my fickle fowl, and life can be grand even when they are simply enjoying pond moments.

In the book of Jeremiah in the Old Testament, we read these words of encouragement:

> So I went down to the potter's house, and I saw him working at the wheel. But the pot he was shaping from the clay was marred in his hands; so the potter formed it into another pot, shaping it as seemed best to him. Then the word of the Lord came to me: 'O house of Israel, can I not do with you as this potter does?' declares the Lord. '**Like clay in the hand of the potter, so are you in my hand.**'

This is what the Lord says: 'Cursed is the one who trusts in man, who depends on flesh for his strength … But blessed is the man who trusts in the Lord, **whose confidence is in him**. He will be like a tree planted by the water that sends out its roots by the stream. **It does not fear when heat comes; its leaves are always green. It has no worries in a year of drought and never fails to bear fruit.**

God gives each of us gifts and skills and opportunities specific to what He is calling us to do. When we compare our faith journey or talents to someone else's to determine if we are "ready" to be used by Him, we are taking God out of the equation. Once we've said YES to Him, there is no checklist to measure our ability to make a difference for His kingdom. We put ourselves on the potter's wheel and let Him mold and shape us. We say YES, walk in obedience, and leave the results to Him.

I wouldn't trade my life of walking with God for anything. Even when I can't find my balance, God is there. His mercy carries me, and His grace holds me together. **God is faithful – always**.

I've renamed my favorite ducks. "Fret's" new name is "Grace." "Tension" is now known as "Peace." "Strive" is my oldest duck, and now she responds to "Enjoy."

Not all my ducks – not even some of my ducks – are in a row.

But they're all in the same pond.

And that feels, well, just right.

23

Get Out There and Dance

I stepped when they kicked. Slid when they swirled. Hopped to the left when they went right. It wasn't pretty, but it was a blast!

It was a weekend retreat with a group of fabulous women. On Saturday night, a few of them spontaneously started line dancing. Let me tell you … they knew what they were doing. They looked good. Not only did they know the steps, but they added the body movements that made them seem very cool. Today's definition of groovy. They had the special arm moves, spins, shakes, and shimmies that were oh, so impressive.

I watched them get started, knowing that I had no clue how to do what they were doing. But I refused to stand on the sidelines and watch. I wanted to dance. I didn't want to watch someone else have fun … **I wanted to be in on the fun.**

What a hoot! Those line dancing women showed up with grace and laughter. I showed up with fear and trembling, which was transformed into accepting their grace and sharing the laughter.

The next morning at our retreat, our event host and speaker, Sue Lennartson, shared her cancer-battling sister's message: DANCE. Don't sit around and wait. Have fun. Move. Live life. TODAY.

Yes. Yes. Yes!

Friend, what if one day you wake up and realize that life is passing you by? You're missing the parade. You pulled yourself out of the game early. You believe God is small, and your prayers confirm that belief. You can feel in your soul that there is more life inside you. But playing it safe has gotten comfortable – no fear of messing up or looking silly. You're standing on the sidelines and watching the fun because you don't know the moves. Or you think your thighs are too chunky. (*Remember, in an earlier story I told you that I believe jiggly underarms and thighs will one day be a fashion statement?*)

Dear, dear friend. It's time to kick some life into your livin'!

Move from sideline-spectator to moment-maker. Don't wait until you are good at something, or have it all figured out, or have your "ducks in a row." Invite moments of laughter and some fun into your world. Pray big prayers and dream big dreams.

Author Sarah Bessey gives us an extra nudge towards living more fully when she shares these words:

> According to a Chinese proverb, 'when sleeping women wake, mountains move' ... We're Shalom Sistas: we are waking up, and now we have mountains to move.

On her wedding day, my friend Sarah placed a sign in the women's restroom on the counter in front of the mirror: "You're already gorgeous. Now get out there and dance!"

Let's say "Yes!" to everything life has to offer, OK? Let's not miss a moment. Get into God's Word and discover how big He really is! Lean in and listen to Him. Follow His lead. He has amazing things planned **for you** that you can't even imagine!

**Go out into the world uncorrupted,
a breath of fresh air...**

**Provide people with a glimpse of good living and
of the living God.**

Step away from the sidelines.

Move the mountains.

Bring the breath of fresh air.

Give the ducks a rest.

Get out there and dance!

Many Thanks

Steve, you are my guy. Your patience amazes me, and your love grounds me. Thank you for showing me how to think more intentionally and more deeply about my faith. I'm so lucky to share my life with you.

Julie Benedict and Lori Charron, what a blast to be sisters! Thank you for all the over-the-top fun, and memorable stories we've lived and shared together. Laughing and spending time with you is just the best.

Our "This is livin'!" prayer team: Holly Zelinsky, Wendie Pett, Mary Miller, and Stephanie Hofhenke. You guys helped me grow into my brave-ness. (*Is that a word? You know what I mean, right?*) Thank you for your prayers, encouragement, time, and for reading my stuff. Our friendships are settled in my soul.

Mary MacDonell Belisle, your words make me so happy. Thank you for helping me bring clarity and even more life to my writing. Your editing rocks!

Stephanie Hofhenke and the String team: For years you have brought color and design to my messages. It is such a joy working with you. What you've done with this book— Wow. Thank you.

There are a lot of books and blogs and writings just waiting to be read. So, to the readers of my words, thank you. The fact that you take time to read my notes of encouragement and books is a gift I do not take for granted. I am so grateful that you pause during your day to connect with me. I am cheering you on—finish the race!

Therefore, since we are surrounded
by such a huge crowd of witnesses to the life of faith,
let us strip off every weight that slows us down,
especially the sin that so easily trips us up.
And let us run with endurance
the race God has set before us.
Hebrews 12:1 NLT

Something Personal

Isn't it fun to get to know a little bit about the person who wrote the book you're reading? That's sometimes the first page I turn to when I'm reading a new book. Well, since I'm curious about that stuff, I thought you might be too. Here's a little more about my story…

I'm a city girl with a Midwest small town heart. I've asked God to meet me in my celebrations and messy places, and He's always shown up. I worked in corporate America and non-profit organizations for a lot of years, leading initiatives and teams that helped take care of the people side of the work. I started my own speaking, writing, and consulting company in 2002.

For six years, my sisters and I were caregivers for our mom. Alzheimer's may have taken away some of her memories, but she never, ever lost her spirit or her trust in God. She died in January of 2020 and we miss her very much. Our dad died in 2003, and it still seems as though it was yesterday when he was walking through the house, exuberantly exclaiming, "This is livin'!" Our parents showed us how to serve God faithfully.

In my blog (GayeLindfors.com/blog), I'll sometimes write about faith and Bible verses that showed up just when I needed them. Other times I'll remind us that Häagen-Dazs ice cream deserves its own special place on the food pyramid and naps can change the world.

I've written a few other books, including *God Girlfriends &*

Chocolate and *This is Livin'! Learning to Move From Messy Moments to Happy Places.* More humor and stories about God's faithfulness! (You can find them on my website and on Amazon.com.)

My husband Steve and I live in St. Paul, MN. Laughing with him and my two sisters is the best thing ever. My nieces and nephews rock my world. "Ooftah" is one of my favorite words and I believe problems are most quickly solved when Hawaiian pizza or chips and salsa show up … or Häagen-Dazs™ ice cream. Football, jazz, small town cafes, and books create some of my Happy Places.

Whether I'm speaking at women's conferences and retreats, writing books, or blogging, I bring a blend of faith, humor, and life stories to **encourage your heart**, **refresh your faith**, and **give you something to giggle about**!

Friend, life is good, and God is faithful. Blessings on you as you gather your ducks and walk in faith. Your story – your life – matters.

Notes

A Note From Gaye

13: "*This is what God says*": Isaiah 43:16, 18-19; *The Message*; emphasis added.

S.O.S. Flares and Faith

17: "*That day when evening came*": Mark 4:35-40.

19: *Meeder*: Kim Meeder, *Encountering Our Wild God: Ways to Experience His Untamable Presence Every Day.* Minneapolis: Chosen Books, 2018, 95.

19: *Evans*: Tony Evans, *CSB Tony Evans Study Bible.* Nashville: Holman Bible Publishers, 2019, 1538.

19: *Moore*: Beth Moore, *Believing God.* Nashville: B&H Publishing Group, 2015, 113, 19.

20: "*Fear not, for I have redeemed you*": Isaiah 43:1-2,5; emphasis added.

Catch a Glimpse

26: "*Go out into the world uncorrupted*": Philippians 2:14-15; *The Message*; emphasis added.

27: "*Jesus replied: Love the Lord your God*": Matthew 22:37-38.

Getting to Know More About Him

31: "*Of all the commandments*": Mark 12:28.

31: "*The most important one*": Mark 12:29-30.

The Day I Lost a Day

39: "*Teach us to number our days aright*": Psalm 90:12.

39: *Morgan*: Robert J. Morgan, *Mastering Life Before It's Too Late: 10 Biblical Strategies for a Lifetime of Purpose.* New York: Howard Books, 2015, 55. Emphasis added.

39: "*So if you're serious about living*": Colossians 3:1-2; *The Message.*

Celebrating the Burpees

43: *Barton*: Dawn Barton, *Laughing Through the Ugly Cry and Finding Unstoppable Joy.* Nashville: Thomas Nelson, 2020, 114-115.

45: "*For we are God's workmanship*": Ephesians 2:10.

Not in Charge

49: "*Come to me*": Matthew 11:28-29; emphasis added.

50: *Chambers*: Oswald Chambers, *My Utmost for His Highest.* Uhrichsville: Barbour and Company, Inc., 1963, 163.

Little Prayers are OK

59: *Larson:* Susie Larson, *"Your Powerful Prayers: Reaching the Heart of God with a Bold and Humble Faith."* Bloomington: Bethany House, 2017, 27. Emphasis added.

59: *"Is there anyplace I can go"*: Psalm 139:7; *The Message.*

60: *"Do not be anxious about anything"*: Philippians 4:6; emphasis added.

Grasshoppers, Alzheimer's, and God

64: *"So that your faith might not rest"*: I Corinthians 2:5.

64: *"Krippayne:* Scott Krippayne, *"Sometimes He calms the storm"*: Retrieved from <https://www.lyrics.com/lyric/30261715/Sometimes+He+Calms+the+Storm>.

65: *"No eye has seen"*: I Corinthians 2:9; emphasis added.

Cheese and Pickle Sandwiches

69: *"This is the day"*: Psalm 118:24.

69: *"In my anguish I cried to the Lord"*: Psalm 118:5,11,12-13.

69: *"Give thanks to the Lord"*: Psalm 118:1,29; emphasis added.

69: *"Ta dah!"*: https://www.dictionary.com/browse/ta-da

70: "*He came so that they may have life*": John 10:10; emphasis added.

71: "*Taste and see that the Lord is good*": Psalm 34:8; emphasis added.

Finding Your Rhythm

77: "*Be strong and courageous*": Deuteronomy 31:8; emphasis added.

77: "*For the Lord God is a sun and shield*": Psalm 84:11; emphasis added.

Breathe. Just Breathe.

81: *Tankersley*: Leeana Tankersley, *Begin Again: The Brave Practice of Releasing Hurt & Receiving Rest.* Grand Rapids: Revell, 2018, 22.

82: "*The ropes of death entangled me*": Psalm 18:4,6,19; NLT.

82: "*I cried out to the Lord*": Psalm 18:6; NLT.

83: "*He reached down from on high and took hold of me*": Psalm 18:19; emphasis added.

Let It Go

88: "*This righteousness from God*": Romans 3:23; NLT; emphasis added.

88: *"Since we've compiled this long and sorry record"*: Romans 3:23; *The Message*; emphasis added.

89: *Peterson*: Eugene H. Peterson, *As Kingfishers Catch Fire: A Conversation on the Ways of God Formed by the Words of God*. Colorado Springs: Waterbrook, 2017, 200.

Something Wonderful is About to Happen

94: *"Why would you ever complain"*: Isaiah 40:27-31; *The Message*; emphasis added.

94: *"You will keep in perfect peace"*: Isaiah 26:3; NLT; emphasis added.

94: *"And I am convinced"*: Romans 8:38-39; NLT; emphasis added.

95: *"Look at the lilies of the field"*: Matthew 6:28-30; NLT; emphasis added.

95: *"Weeping may last through the night"*: Psalm 30:5; NLT; emphasis added.

95: *"I will never forget"*: Lamentations 3:20-23; NLT; emphasis added.

My Finguh Hurts

100: *"The goal is to bring out the best in others"*: Colossians 4:6; *The Message*; emphasis added.

100: *"Therefore, as God's chosen people"*: Colossians 3:12,14; emphasis added.

101: *Carmichael*: Amy Carmichael, *If*. Fort Washington: CLC Publications, Original publication 1938, Revised edition 2011, 7.

Kickin' Butt

106: *The Israelites were fighting one of their biggest rivalries*: See I Samuel 13.

107: "*Jonathan said to his young armor-bearer*": I Samuel 14:6.

107: "*There's no rule that says*": I Samuel 14:6; *The Message*; emphasis added.

108: "*Royal position for such a time as this*": Esther 4:14.

108: "*If you throw us in the fire*": Daniel 3:17-18; *The Message*; emphasis added.

108: *Lindfors*: Gaye Lindfors, *God Girlfriends & Chocolate: Encouraging Stories from the Heart*. Independently published, Amazon Kindle Direct Publishing, 2010, 90.

110: "*Ah, Sovereign Lord*": Jeremiah 32:17; emphasis added.

110: "*Now to him who is able to do far more*": Ephesians 3:20; emphasis added.

110: "*Fear not, for I am with you*": Isaiah 41:10; emphasis added.

The Rut Has to Go

114: "*See, I am doing a new thing*": Isaiah 43:19; emphasis added.

Life Whisperers

119: "*Do you remember the Bible story*": See Numbers 13.

120: "*But the people who live there are powerful*": Numbers 13:28.

120: "*We should go up*" Number 13:30.

120: "*Twelve Men Went to Spy on Canaan.*" Retrieved from https://mygrandmatime.com/3019-2/visit-with-grandma/sing-with-grandma/12-men-went-to-spy-on-canaan.

121: "*They spread among the Israelites a bad report*": Numbers 13:32.

121: "*Where can we go*": Deuteronomy 1:28; emphasis added.

122: *Chambers*: Oswald Chambers, *My Utmost for His Highest*. Uhrichsville: Barbour and Company, Inc., 1963, 134. Emphasis added.

122: "*Your own ears will hear him*": Isaiah 30:21; NLT.

122: "*My sheep listen to my voice*": John 10:27.

123: "*Speak, Lord*": I Samuel 3:10.

When the Parade Passes By

129: "*This is the day the Lord has made*": Psalm 118:24; emphasis added.

Grace, Mercy, Love, and Dignity

133: "*At dawn he [Jesus] appeared again*": John 8:1-11.

135: "*Love the Lord your God*": Matthew 22:37-39; emphasis added.

Finish the Race

138: Meredith Williams, *Chicken Fat Song*. Retrieved from <https://genius.com/Robert-preston-chicken-fat-lyrics>.

140: "*Therefore, since we are surrounded*": Hebrews 12:1; *NLT;* emphasis added.

141: "*Do you see what this means*": Hebrews 12:1; *The Message*; emphasis added.

Getting My Ducks in a Row. Or Not.

145: "*So I went down to the potter's house*": Jeremiah 18:3-6; emphasis added.

146: "*This is what the Lord says*": Jeremiah 17:5, 7-8; emphasis added.

Get Out There and Dance!

149: *Bessey*: Sarah Bessey, Quoted in Osheta Moore, *Shalom Sistas: Living Wholeheartedly in a Brokenhearted World*. Harrisonburg: Herald Press, 2017, 13,15.

150: "*Go out into the world uncorrupted*": Philippians 2:15; *The Message*; emphasis added.

Life is Good!

Sharing my thoughts when capturing life happenings that I find amusing, reconciling my faith with the real world and giggling about "You've got to be kidding me" moments.

Books by Gaye

God, Girlfriends, & Chocolate

This is Livin'! Learning to Move from Messy Moments to Happy Places

You can find these books at

GayeLindfors.com/books or Amazon.com

Let's Connect!

Hello, Friend!

We all have ducks that we're trying to get into a row, right? Or at least into the same pond?

Let's stay connected so we can remind each other that we are not alone when we are trying to gather those duckies, and there's always someone cheering us on!

If you're receiving my weekly notes of encouragement, whoo hoo! If you aren't, ooftah! Each message is intended to **refresh your faith** and **deliver some joy**. Just click the link on my website to stay connected this way—easy peasy.

www.GayeLindfors.com

Facebook: @GayeLindforsAuthor

Instagram: @GayeLindfors

LinkedIn: @GayeLindfors

Made in USA - Kendallville, IN
1199711_9798562646606
11.25.2020 1350